“I count Kristin Beasle
her heart. *Who Do You*

women discover the freedom, joy, and significance the Scriptures teach. It is grounded in biblical truth and wisdom that touches the heart. Both men and women will profit from reading this book.”

—Dr. Norman G. Wakefield,
Professor Emeritus of Pastoral Theology, Phoenix Seminary

“What an amazing gift to bask in the words, reality, and truth of this great book—a book for every Christian woman. Words that represent the truth of God’s infinite, highest, and best plan for woman … to be ‘His female image bearers.’ With such a calling as this, Kristin Beasley weaves the vision and challenge of our privileged position in Kingdom work, for His glory alone, powerfully and masterfully.”

—Naomi Rhode, *CSP, CPAE Speaker Hall of Fame, Cofounder of SmartHealth*

“Dr. Beasley has written an excellent study on the value of women. It is founded in the Scriptures and offers biblical solutions for those plagued with issues related to their worth and value to God and others. I highly recommend this study to both women and men.”

—T. Kem Oberholtzer, Ph.D.
President/Founder Grace Rock Ministries The Woodlands, Texas

DR. KRISTIN BEASLEY
with JODI CARLSON

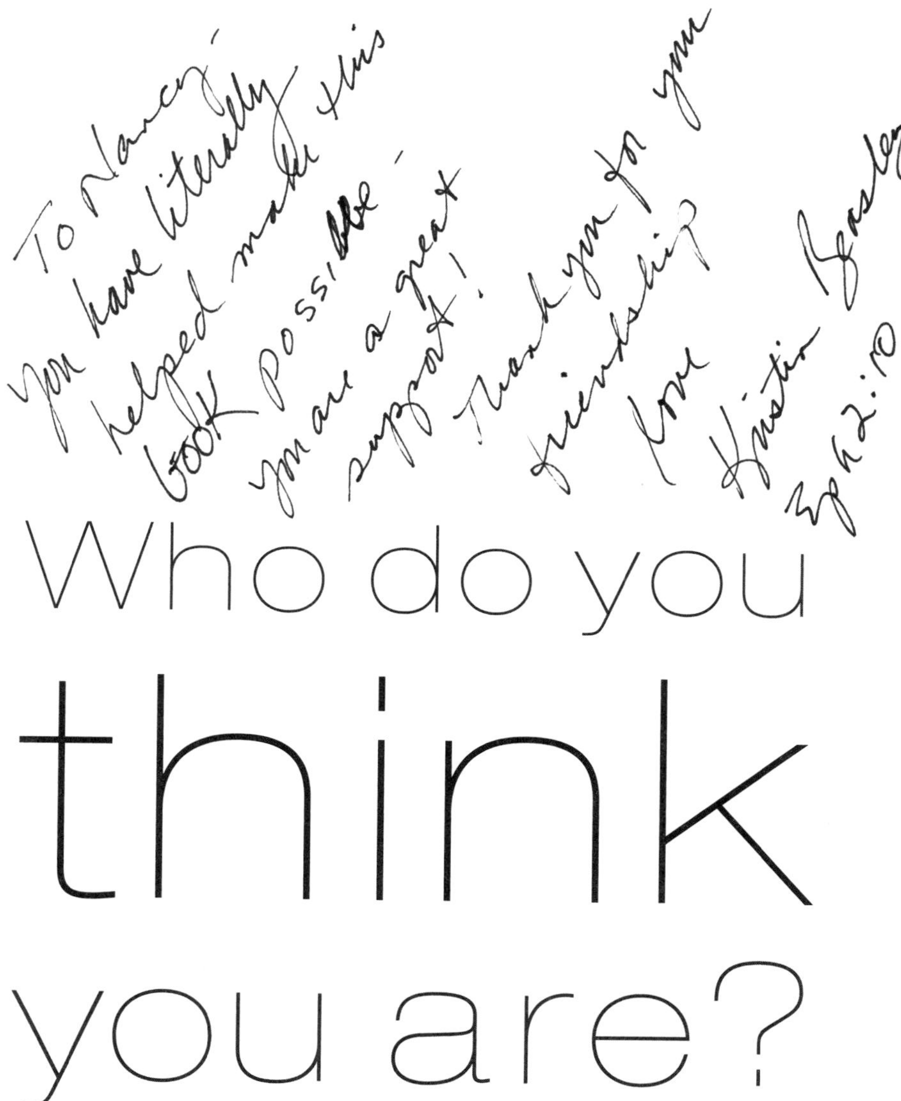

Who do you think you are?

GOOD NEWS ABOUT YOUR IDENTITY

Who do you

think

you are?

Who Do You Think You Are?
Published by Kristin Beasley

For information:
Greater Reach Ministries
8283 N. Hayden Road
Suite 258
Scottsdale, AZ 85258
www.greaterreach.com
ISBN (cloth): 978-1-61658-555-6
ISBN (paper): 978-1-61658-556-3

Printed in the United States of America
5 4 3 2 1 / 2010 2011 2012 2013

This book is dedicated to:

My husband, Fred, who encouraged (and encourages) me, fixed me coffee, fed me, and all in all made sure I stayed on track and finished this project. You inspire me!

And to all the women who have struggled
to feel more than "less than."
This book is for you.

If people can't see what God is doing,
they stumble all over themselves;
But when they attend to what he reveals,
they are most blessed.
—Proverbs 29:18 (MSG)

Contents

Acknowledgments

Over the years there have been many people who have helped me with the insights, encouragement, and feedback that have guided the development of this book. I am deeply grateful to them all. There are some, however, that I want to specifically mention.

My husband, Fred, who has been a help in so many ways, a collaborator, friend, cheerleader, and strong protector. Thanks for reading this so often you have it memorized.

Steve and Barbara Uhlmann, who have invested in me and my ministry for many years. They are generous and prayerful friends and supporters.

My Greater Reach staff: Alyssa, Caye, Mari, Nancy.

The Greater Reach Ministries Board and prayer team. Thank you all for believing in me, this ministry, and this project. I could not do this alone. You show me how the Body of Christ is supposed to work.

Jodi Carlson, who worked so hard collaborating with me in getting this book written—thank you for your creativity, commitment to timing, and helpful insights! I need people like you in my life!

Lisa Ham, for all the technical support. You kept me on the "straight and narrow."

Norm Wakefield, Kem Oberholtzer, and Naomi Rhode, for telling me years ago I should do this.

Acknowledgments

Part One

The Value of a Woman

On one particular island in the South Pacific, a man could purchase a wife with cows. Yes, cows. That was the custom. If the woman was really beautiful and outstanding, she could win her father as many as five or six cows. If she was nice and pleasant looking, maybe four cows. If she was average and not much to look at, three.

A farmer on this island had two daughters of marriageable age. One was beautiful, the other very, very plain. A rich young man came to the island to buy a wife, and he sought out the farmer, knowing about his single daughters. This man wanted to meet them so that he could choose one and take home his bride. Certainly, the plain daughter might bring the farmer two cows, but more likely one. The farmer thought the rich man would surely want the beautiful daughter, so he planned to negotiate five or even six cows for her.

Who do you think you are?

However, when the rich man arrived, he had eyes only for the plain daughter. In fact, he was so set on her that he paid the farmer nothing short of ten cows. Ten!

They married, went on their honeymoon, and two years later came back to visit. My, how she had changed. Once gangly, homely, and awkward, this woman was now well poised and quite lovely. She glowed with contentment. She had become a ten-cow woman because her husband thought she was a ten-cow woman.[1]

How could such a transformation be possible? Is it that a man holds the power to change a woman from the inside out? Or is it that each and every woman, regardless of male input, becomes a reflection of her perceived value?

What's your value as a woman in today's society? Your answer will depend on whom you listen to. Brothers, sisters, moms and dads. Television, billboards, radio, ads. Friends, teachers, acquaintances, politicians. Books, magazines, movies, the Internet. Our world and culture send an overload of mixed messages. Is a woman a commodity, a sexual plaything, a baby-bearing housewife? Is her value found in her appearance, her gender, the roles she fulfills? Is she valuable at all?

What *is* your value?

Who do you think you are?

If you hold this book in your hands because you seek answers to fundamental questions about who you are, what it means to be a woman, what is your true value, or why in the world you're here, I have good news for you. You are worth more than cows, more than even ten cows. Your value is actually beyond tangible measure. And you exist for a specific reason.

You may not know it. You may not feel it. Or perhaps you know it but you certainly don't feel it. *It* is the truth that you are loved, significant, and gifted. *It* is the truth that you are called to a life of meaning, value, and purpose. *It* is not that you have value because of anything you do or don't do, but that you are valuable because Someone has deemed you valuable.

I did not originate the core truths in these pages. But I have discovered them and have sought to live them. And now I give them to you. I hope this book is a tool that will clarify the truth for you. The truth, should you choose to accept it, is entirely yours to claim. And the transformed life that will result is entirely yours to live …

Chapter 1

What's the Problem?

Thrilled with my birthday gift, I rushed to the wall where it hung the first morning. There it was … the Mirror. Not just any mirror, this was *the* Mirror on the Wall—that very truth-telling mirror that the queen gazed at when she heard those dread words, "Oh Lady Queen, though fair ye be, Snow White is fairer far than thee." Secure in the knowledge that Disney's Snow White, at seventy-two, would surely no longer be in the running, I bravely stepped before the omniscient oracle of beauty.

"Mirror, Mirror, on the wall, any chance I'm even close to the top one thousand fairest of them all?"

It answered:

"Dear Lady, though I gaze at thee, thy mother's face is all I see."

Startled awake, in full sweat and relieved it was only a dream, I rolled over to sneak a few more winks as my own prince snored away.

What do you see when you look in the mirror? What do you think about what you see? Do you ever think, *How did that happen?!*

When we look in the mirror, more often than not we see our flaws. Blemishes we wish would go away, aging that has us worn and haggard, a nose too broad, wrinkles too numerous, a hairdo too boring. Many mornings I am aghast at the repair work I have to do before I can meet the world for the day.

As I get older, I try to encourage myself to have a sense of humor about the changes staring back at me. I try to remind myself: outer appearance is *not* all there is; I am *not* a huge reclamation project;

how we look is one of the *least* important things about us. After all, in some cultures the manifestations of old age are signs of honor deserving reverence and respect for a life that has survived and grown in wisdom. In the United States, however, we are encouraged every day to fight aging and cover it up. We are bombarded with the message that appearance is everything for today's woman. So, we clothe, color, accessorize, work out, suck in, push up, slim down, bleach, inject, nip and tuck our bodies into submission. Or we try to ignore our image altogether, covering ourselves in plus, double plus, and triple plus.

But more often than not, what we notice in the mirror isn't whether we need to fix our hair, teeth, shape, or skin. What we see lies far deeper than physical features. What we see is what we *really believe* about ourselves. No matter the face, what many of us see is a not-so-lovable person. Someone "less than." Someone who just doesn't quite measure up. Some even see an outright failure.

What do you see when you look in the mirror? Whether young or old, mother or not, married or single, professional or not, do you see someone with infinite value? Someone who is lovable, precious, and gifted? Do you see a life being lived as a crucial part of an eternal plan?

Likely not, particularly first thing in the morning.

> What we see is what we
> *really believe* about ourselves.

Can You Relate?

I had lunch not long ago with a young professional woman who was trying to find her niche. What she really wants is to be married, but a few years ago she suffered through an abusive relationship and now relationships are very difficult for her. In lieu of marriage she is pursuing a career. She never imagined she would be single this long, and it really bothers her. She is beginning to realize that since marriage probably will not happen in the near future, she needs to plan seriously for a life on her own.

I told her the truth. I told her that she is valuable just the way she is, as God's unique creation. Did she hear me? Yes. But did she believe me? No. She feels as though something is wrong with her. I talked to her about this book, which was then in its early stages. I told her about the true value of a woman and the source of her authentic, eternal, God-given value. I told her that I have observed how hard it is for women to get the truth about their value to go from mere intellectual head knowledge into the heart, penetrating the core of one's being. Suddenly her eyes welled with tears and she said, "I wish it weren't so hard." Deep inside, she said, she felt flawed and "less than."

This woman is missing an internalized knowledge of her true value. This young woman—educated, attractive, engaging, and articulate—has the advantage of knowing Jesus Christ. She knows in her head that God's Word says she is valuable and has an important role to play in this world, but she doesn't *feel* that way. She knows she is supposed to believe His truth, but her doubts get in the way of experiencing that truth.

I have seen this attitude among bright, college-educated American women more times than I can count. I have observed it in women who populate every level of society, represent the entire spectrum of educational achievement, and even come from various cultures around the world. In ministry trips abroad I have encountered women on every continent who feel "less than." A well-educated pastor's wife from Hong Kong attended one of my classes and said, "I didn't know that others all over the world have carried the burden I have carried, too. My Chinese culture has put so much on women. Really, the whole world has hurt women deeply. I thought I was the only one. I can't believe I have never learned this before."

This is the plight of hundreds of millions of Middle Eastern, Romanian, Russian, African, Indian, Pakistani, Afghani, Chinese, South American, and, yes, American women today.

A Ceaseless War

A war is being waged against women today. It does not discriminate based on abuse or emotional health, wealth or poverty, race or creed. Women everywhere are often confused and too often denied the truth about who they really are. Misinformation dominates. Lies prevail. Discouragement sets in. The assumption that women are inferior, "less than," insignificant, or worthless screams louder than the truth. The truth is almost unrecognizable because its light is dimmed by a thousand dark lies.

Women around the world desperately need to hear the truth. What is the truth? Would you believe me if I told you I was telling you the truth? Thank God, you don't have to believe a word *I* say! My words will not stand forever, into eternity, but God's will. His Word—His Truth—has been reality since before there was time, and it will remain long after you and I pass away (1 Pet. 1:25).

The truth that He wants you to know and experience is this: You, woman, are valuable. You, woman, are loved. You, woman, are a wonderful creation. And you, woman, are designed with a greater purpose than you can imagine. (See John 3:16; Ps. 139:13–16; Ps. 8:4–6; Eph. 2:10.)

This truth needs to be told over and over again because we don't get it; we don't believe it. We don't believe that the Truth is actually true. We must not, for if we did it would move us to focus more on what we see than how we look; we would act based upon what we know more than how we feel; we would trade cowering for confidence and live the Truth out loud.

Maybe you have never been taught that you are valuable. Maybe you have always been told, directly or indirectly, that you are subpar … that you are "less than," particularly next to men. Maybe you have been taught for so long that your only value lies in your ability to produce and raise children. If no husband is on the horizon, or if perhaps your children are now grown, you feel your value has vanished.

How we need truth! Women need to hear, study, believe, and live out the truth about our incomparable value, dignity, and significance. To fail to do so is to shortchange the world, disrespect our Creator, and miss much of what we are meant to live out.

A Completely Christian Worldview

We need a cosmic mind change. The lack of value toward women needs to be addressed worldwide. And frankly, multitudes of Christian men and women around the world are part of the problem. They perpetuate the attitude that women are "less than."

Consistently negative views of women abound in churches all over the world. I can't think of one church or school I have encountered where a negative view of women is not possessed by at least some, if not most, of the people. In Jordan I was speaking with a woman, a Christian national, about marriages among the Christians in her country. Knowing that wife beating is acceptable in the Muslim culture, I said, "Surely, Christian marriages are in better shape here."

To my horror she replied that no, Christian marriages are so influenced by Muslim culture that wife beatings are common in the church. She longs to see this changed and the status of women elevated to that of her Christian brothers. In order for that to happen, men need their minds changed by the Word of God. They need a more complete Christian worldview, one that includes valuing women, their sisters in Christ.

Nancy Pearcey, in her book *Total Truth,* said our worldview is not to be used "just as of a set of coherent ideas, but also as a blueprint for living. Believers need a roadmap for a full and consistent Christian life."[1] According to Pearcey, most Christians have a worldview that is only partially Christian. The Jordanian Christian men in my friend's congregation have a Christian worldview that is incomplete. They hold a belief about women that is influenced by the culture in which they live. And it is not a Christian culture. They may be Christians, but they don't think or behave like godly Christian husbands when they beat and devalue their wives. Their worldview, how they perceive the world, is a mixture of Christian thinking, Muslim practice, and cultural acceptance. They need their minds renewed (Rom. 12:1–2) so that they think biblically about women and the marriage relationship. Only then will they act appropriately, their behavior being transformed into that of a true Christ follower.

What about us? We may have a Christian worldview about the creation of the world, or about the lordship of Christ, but what about our personal value? If we don't value ourselves, if we fail to grasp our God-given worth, we don't have a fully Christian worldview. If we separate the spiritual from the secular, or acknowledge that God is good and loves His children but think that we are somehow an exception, then we're not living out a fully Christian worldview.

Biblically there is no separation of the secular and the spiritual. All of life is holy. And all of humanity is of incomparable worth … including you.

One of my female seminary students wrote in a paper, "I have always thought men are better than women." Another said she is puzzled by "how the Christian community has distorted woman's value and purpose in the same way as has the secular world." I have had men in my seminary classes tell me that men are superior to women because they are not as emotional or talkative, and that men are more competent. While these are certainly generalizations, they are beliefs that have come from faulty assumptions. Our assumptions, whether correct or incorrect, form the beliefs that construct our worldview. We'll look at assumptions more closely in the next chapter.

In North America women have a hard time being taken seriously, whether inside or outside of the church. The full-time homemaker is underrated, and her experience is counted as irrelevant in searching for a "real" job. Though there has been some improvement, women still tend to be paid less than men for the same work in the marketplace. We need a cosmic mind change. This book is a call to arms for a worldwide shift in thinking regarding the value of women. *And it starts with you!*

You, woman, are valuable.

The Whole Truth and Nothing but the Truth

This book covers an important topic: you. Together, we are going to dust off that old mirror, hold it up, and examine what you believe you see. Then, we'll hold up the *true* mirror, the mirror that sees

Christ in us—the Bible—to learn the *objective* truth, and discover how to make *the* truth *your* truth.

In our postmodern culture, objective truth is dismissed. Personal reality or personal truth is touted as being acceptable, and objective truth—reality!—is rejected. Objective truth, as detailed in the pages of this book, is critical for us to grasp in order to become fully who God made us to be. Emotional experiences have burned negative assumptions and beliefs into our minds and hearts. These must be replaced with *true* Truth—Truth that comes from the mouth of God.

Without God's truth we are left to flounder. We develop theology regarding the identity and value of women from secular thinking, wrong or shallow biblical understanding, false assumptions developed early in life, past experiences, or others' opinions of us. And in the end, we have no help finding our way.

The time to speak the truth is now because it is always the right time to speak truth. The truth about who we are and who God is must be told over and over again, repeated and reiterated. Often we don't understand it, or we hesitate to believe it because perhaps it simply seems too good to be true.

In order for the truth about intrinsic value and true identity to be lived out, it must first be embraced. It must be internalized. It must become a pattern of thought. Then it can become living, breathing … *real.* You can own it, feel it, and make choices based upon it. Once internalized, this truth is the ticket to freedom from the bondage of hateful, destructive, and even seemingly "white" lies. The truth has the power to break the chains of wrong beliefs that hold us—unaware—in a prison of self-defeat.

And what is this truth? The truth is that women are precious and valuable to God. Women are equally as important and loved as their male counterparts. The truth is: *You* have unimaginable value in God's sight. You are significant, unique, and beautifully designed. Your value is not tied to any role you must perform, but to your very personhood. It's about who you are. It has nothing to do with what you do.

Many books are written about women's roles. This book is about who you *are*. Women are created in God's image. For that reason alone, women are valuable. We have the opportunity to reflect Him no matter what we do in life. To be a roving ambassador in this world for the Most High God is an awesome gift and calling.

This truth is not hidden in Scripture. It is obvious. Yet we miss it time and again. I know I did for a long time. If you find yourself discouraged, dispirited, or hopeless today, read this book. It will be a blessing to you, inspiring you and encouraging you with fresh hope. I want to give you practical ways to begin living the truth of your inherent value. And I want to challenge you to live out your calling, to unapologetically live and thrive as a woman of God! There is no greater end for which to live out the days of your life on earth.

If there's something deep within you that recognizes the truth of your eternal significance but you just don't know how to take hold of it, read on, my friend. This book is for you!

Prayer

Lord God, I need You. I know You say one thing about my identity, and I confess that I am far from truly believing it. I want to align myself with Your truth—not just once, but all the days of my life. I want it to ring true not just in my head, but in my heart and soul. I want the abundant life that You want for me. As I read this book, reveal Yourself to me. Change me and make me new. Guide me through this process. Amen.

Chapter 2

The Power of Assumptions

By the time we boarded the plane I was walking on my last nerve, scanning each and every passenger to make sure they "looked safe." All was well in my eyes until a man of Middle Eastern descent sat directly across the aisle from my husband and me. He looked grumpy. He kept his head bowed. He would not make eye contact. My heart began to race …

We had been looking forward to this trip for more than a year. Fred and I were to co-teach a seminary class in Jordan. The myriad tasks in preparing for a ministry trip to the Middle East had been scrutinized and accomplished, their boxes neatly checked off. The flights were booked, the hotels arranged, transportation secured, and the students registered. Every minute detail had been covered. Except one. Granted, it was not a detail we could have foreseen, but it made all of the other details of our trip irrelevant in its wake. It was September 15, 2001, mere days after the 9/11 attacks.

If you remember those days after the attack on the World Trade Center and the Pentagon and the foiled attack on the Capitol, you recall that life immediately became more insecure than ever before for Americans. Hotels were empty. Flights were cancelled. Conventions and vacations were shelved. Everyone in the United States was jittery about flying, terrorist attacks, and—truth be told—people of Middle Eastern descent.

Then there's Fred.

My husband is by nature adventurous and trusting. He prayerfully determined that we should follow through and not let "a few evil people" frighten us away from God's will. But I was nervous. Honestly, I did not want to go. I wanted to hide out at home, play it safe. But I knew Fred was right about trusting God, and I agreed to follow through.

And now we were seated right across the aisle from the person I was sure would make us all news media fodder. Was it unusual for someone who looked like they were from the Middle East to board a plane that was heading that direction? No. But did he stand out to me? Yes. I zeroed in on him. He continued to avert his gaze from others. His facial features, once grumpy, now looked menacing to me. *Not on my flight, mister.* With thumping chest, I began to muster my "Let's Roll" plan.

Meanwhile, my husband, oblivious to my increasing angst, was struggling to get his computer working. Just then, the Middle Eastern man reached under his seat and made a quick motion to pull something out. Close to a coronary, I told my body to lunge forward protectively across my unwitting beloved. The words *He has a bomb!* screamed inside my head. But fear had petrified every sinew and my lips were glued shut. The result was a kind of twitch and a dry raspy cough ... as the man pulled out his laptop. The foolishness I felt dissolved into shame as he leaned over and offered his computer to Fred to use.

Yes, I was ashamed. I had made so many assumptions so quickly and so effortlessly, and all of them were wrong! I thought this man looked mean and unfriendly. I thought he was reaching for something dangerous. I thought we were being threatened. Though no one knew at that moment what I was thinking, my face was red with embarrassment.

God revealed my prejudice in that instant. I had judged someone by the color of his skin. I had long prided myself on not being prejudiced against people because of how they looked, yet I had responded to the way this man looked. I had drawn some very wrong conclusions. As the plane raced down the runway, my heart still raced, too. But this time my heart ran to God's throne, humbled and hungry for forgiveness.

My wrong belief was so deeply internalized that I didn't recognize it before that moment. (In fact, I had been justifying it.) My belief was driving my thinking, and my thinking was driving my behavior. My quickened pulse, paranoid glances, and sweaty palms testified against me. I had intellectually embraced the idea of not discriminating against people, but here I was, in fact practicing discrimination.

It's often hard to see the dichotomy between our verbalized beliefs and our deeply rooted internalized beliefs with such clarity. It may take an "aha" experience like the one I had to see what is *really* going on inside. But it's these internalized beliefs and assumptions that motivate and shape our attitudes, actions, and decisions. They are indeed powerful, for they guide our everyday living. To change our everyday lifestyle, we must unearth and examine our assumptions.

Is What We *Really* Believe *Really* True?

The way we think and the conclusions we draw deeply affect how we live our lives. Consider the Christian woman—you may be one of them—who readily states, "Yes, I am valuable because God says I am," but a closer look at her life reveals a low self-esteem and sense of value. She has "head knowledge" of the truth that she is worthy of love and respect, but her internal assumptions oppose her verbalized beliefs. And what we truly believe in our heart of hearts is what is lived out in our lives.

The problem is, our internalized beliefs are often not the truth! Our beliefs commonly spring from emotional experience. Emotional experience is very powerful and easily believed as truth. So we make assumptions about ourselves based on wrong information, and emotional experience in turn becomes our truth … our reality.

I have a good Christian friend who is married to a good Christian man. Together they raised two children, a boy and a girl, doing the best they could to raise them to be well-rounded, godly people. My friends were attentive parents, loving, and not overly permissive or restrictive. They spent a lot of time with their kids. By anyone's standard they were great parents.

To change our everyday lifestyle, we must unearth and examine our assumptions.

But what do you think happened when their daughter became pregnant at age eighteen by someone she had no intention of marrying? My friend said, "I always assumed that young girls who get pregnant when they're not married must have received poor parenting … until *my* daughter got pregnant." She was not aware of her own assumption until it flew up in her face.

What is an assumption? It is something we accept as true, and take for granted to be true, based on likely evidence; a supposition. Assumptions are typically unobtrusive and comfortable, and they help us make sense of the world. By their very nature assumptions are powerful, influencing all that we are. The danger is that assumptions may not be true at all, yet they can shape our worldview—the way we view, live, and interact in our environment. Consider the story of Fraiser from Lisuland in north Burma.

> [Fraiser] translated the Scriptures into the Lisu language and then left a young fellow with the task of teaching the people to read. When he returned six months later, he found three students and the teacher seated around a table, with the Scriptures opened in front of the teacher. When the students each read, they left the Bible where it was. The man on the left read it sideways, the man on the right read it sideways but from the other side, and the man across from the teacher read it upside down. Since they always occupied the same chairs, that's how each had learned to read, and that's how each thought the language was written.[1]

This story reveals just how "off" an assumption can be. Each student assumed he was seeing the language as it was intended to be read. But Lisu, as with every language, has letters and symbols created to be read and comprehended from one angle only. In this story, only the teacher saw the language from the correct perspective as it was intended to be read. The same applies to us: There is only one true angle from which we are to view ourselves—God's. But how often do we default to our own perspective, which is so often completely upside down from His?

The Origin of Assumptions

Assumptions are birthed early in life. As children we are unaware that they are taking shape. Through both verbal and nonverbal input and feedback from those around us, we develop assumptions about ourselves. We carry them with us, and with the passage of time they turn into deep-seated beliefs that color our sense of value.

And they can be very difficult to root out. Notice I said *can*. It is not impossible, for "all things are possible with God" (Mark 10:27).

As we grow older, we may receive messages that don't fit with our original assumptions. Rather than live with the uncomfortable feeling that this contrary information creates, we often dismiss the new information—even if it's true.

Perhaps you were raised being told you were stupid and had nothing to contribute. You likely made an assumption about these hurtful statements—that they were true. You believed them. As much pain as these abusive comments caused, they became a part of your worldview. As the years have gone by, no matter how many times people told you, "You can do it" and "You are bright," you still don't believe it. You have allowed an emotional experience to trump objective truth. I know two people very well who have struggled with this lie. One has not let it stop her from learning and developing; the other is still stuck living a lie. (We will look closely at the objective truth about your value in Part Two of this book.)

It's hard to completely embrace something that's contrary to our original assumptions, let alone learn to function based on that truth. To help us pinpoint our false assumptions, it helps to consider how and where we first developed them. There are several originations, including but not limited to the following sources.

1. Faulty thinking

If an athlete signs up to run a relay race by himself without knowing the definition of a relay race (that it's a team sport), he automatically fails before he begins. By definition, no one can win a relay race alone. His assumption that he can run and even win a relay race as a solo runner is not based on fact. Due to faulty thinking, he automatically sets himself up to fail.

2. Culture

Assumptions, right or wrong, can come from our culture. The Maasai, an African tribe in Tanzania with which our church has a growing relationship, believe that leaving human or animal feces along the pathways instead of buried underground will protect one's spirit. Not surprisingly, they have serious hygiene problems in their culture. Their assumption fails to consider the reality of disease, and they suffer the physical ramifications.

3. Superstition

Assumptions can come from superstition, a belief in the significance of something that is not rooted in reason or knowledge. They are silly to those who do not subscribe to them, but to those who do, superstitions alter their patterns, habits, and life as a whole. For example, those who believe in astrological signs rely on their horoscopes to predict the future. Based on whatever their horoscopes say, they may avoid doing something on a particular day, repeat a certain behavior, or constantly be on the lookout for something to happen. Assumptions based on superstition keep us from living in reality.

4. Limited perspective

A limited perspective can breed false assumptions. If a worker fails to see beyond the present day and plan for retirement, he will spend all he earns today and not save any money for his future. This limited perspective will not show itself as a problem right now, but it will when he retires. A limited perspective keeps us from seeing the whole picture, and the whole picture is reality.

5. History

Assumptions can come from history. People assumed the Earth was the center of our solar system until Nicolaus Copernicus discovered the reality—the truth that the Earth revolves around the sun. Of course, nobody believed him at first. But now, in light of the truth, science has expanded and we have made tremendous strides in space exploration, weather forecasts, and more because we have a correct understanding of Earth's place in the solar system.

6. Family background and values

My parents, adults in my church, and my teachers were always trying to reign in my talkativeness. I assumed they thought I didn't have anything of value to say. I thought they were implying that my opinion didn't count, that I wasn't very bright, that I should be "seen but not heard." I didn't realize they were just trying to get a break from my constant jabbering! I saw my false belief play out later in life when, as a new faculty member at Phoenix Seminary, I struggled to find the courage and confidence to speak up in meetings.

I had internalized a belief that had developed from a wrong assumption. Mary Belenky, in her book *Women's Ways of Knowing,* says, "All women grow up having to deal with historically and culturally ingrained definitions of femininity and womanhood—one common theme being that women, like children, should be seen and not heard."[2] Her comments came out of extensive research that she and other contributors to her book had done regarding how women think and see themselves. You can imagine how surprised I was to discover I wasn't the only woman who had carried this wrong belief into adulthood.

The Results of False Assumptions

Everyone's thinking and behaviors are inextricably tied to their beliefs. The Bible says, "As he thinketh in his heart, so is he" (Prov. 23:7, KJV). The implications of this simple truth are staggering, particularly as it relates to our own sense of value. Who we think we are shapes us!

When we have a painful emotional experience, we women often blame ourselves. We assume we are at fault. This is easy to do, and we do it all the time. Suppose you put on your favorite jeans one day, only to discover that they are too tight for you. Do you say to yourself, *I need to go on a diet,* or do you say, *These jeans shrunk*? (I have had personal experience with this problem! Confession: I don't blame the jeans!)

Women tend to point inward when things go wrong. Men tend to point outward. When jilted by a friend or lover, we think we are worthless. We think *we* are the problem. That is not true. We may bear some responsibility in a relationship that goes wrong, but it actually takes two to have a problem. It is almost universally true that no one person is totally to blame for the deterioration or severance of a relationship.

Having a relationship problem has nothing to do with your value as a woman created in the image of God. But we believe we are worthless because we've had a deeply painful experience. We made an assumption from that experience that then formed the basis of a belief. When we believe a lie, it impacts our behavior, our decisions, and ultimately our life's course.

This phenomenon accounts for one reason why so many women stay in abusive relationships. The woman assumes she is the one to blame, and she believes deep down that she doesn't deserve any better. She may believe she is powerless. These are assumptions rooted in the misperception that she lacks personal value. These assumptions come from faulty thinking.

Our beliefs stem from our assumptions, and they can have a negative impact—if not devastating results—on our entire lives if they are not true. Consider how false assumptions can impact us. Among many other ways, they can:

- narrow our view of reality;
- limit our understanding of truth;
- influence our choices and behavior;
- misguide our attitudes;
- influence our thinking about right and wrong;
- block effective communication;
- cause us to miss out on the abundant life God intends for us.

I know a woman who was born with a mild-to-moderate hearing loss. That means she can function well in the world with hearing aids; she does not need to communicate by sign language. Now in her thirties, this woman is successful in her career, has many wonderful friends, and has a solid relationship with Jesus Christ. Even though she grew up just as privileged as the children around her—with a great education, a loving family, and material blessings—she always sensed she was different from the "normal" kids, those who had full hearing. She assumed her hearing aids separated her and made her "less than."

When we believe a lie,
it impacts our behavior, our
decisions, and ultimately
our life's course.

She did not realize this assumption until, in her twenties, she analyzed her behavior. She noticed that she would wait for people to put her down. Because she didn't think she was worthy of love and companionship, she became keenly aware of negative feedback. Perfectionism took over as she tried to prove herself to the world, all the while believing in her core that she was unworthy. Do you see how a false assumption about herself misguided her overall attitude, influenced her behavior on a daily basis, and caused her to miss out on abundant living?

This woman would be the first to confess that she believes the Bible is God's infallible Word. The Bible is clear that she is of such great worth that God gave His one and only Son's life for her because He loves her (John 3:16). So, by professing one thing with her mouth and believing another in her heart, this woman does what I had done in the story at the beginning of this chapter. She lives with a chasm between what she says she believes and what she actually believes and lives out.

If we take an honest look at our assumptions, very few of us would discover that we truly think completely biblically about our personal identity. Would any of us consciously adopt a belief that we know to be false? No way! False assumptions mess with our lives. The problem is that usually, deep down, we believe our assumptions are correct.

Trying to change outward attitudes and behavior does very little good in the long run if we fail to examine the basic assumptions that underlie and prompt our behaviors, attitudes, and choices. I like how Stephen Covey puts it: "The more aware we are of our basic paradigms, maps or assumptions, and the extent to which we have been influenced by our experience, the more we can take responsibility for those paradigms, examine them, test them against reality, listen to others and be open to their perceptions, thereby getting a larger picture, and a far more objective view."[3]

Excavating Our Assumptions

So, how do we move forward? The second and third parts of this book will help you embrace your true identity, but before that can happen, you must first identify the faulty assumptions you hold. Who do your assumptions tell you that you are? The study questions in the back of this book will help you think about and identify the negative messages you currently believe about yourself. Please take some time right now to prayerfully respond to the first four Questions for Reflection for chapter 2 found in the back of this book. Then come back to this page.

After some of your assumptions have been pinpointed, in order to change them, you must *want* to correct them and align them with the truth. I of course want this for you and God wants it for you, but even that is not enough. *You* have to want it for yourself. You have to value His truth—*the* truth—above your own. You must invite God into your healing process. If this resonates with you, and it's something you want, now is the time to excavate your faulty assumptions.

First, you must agree to establish Scripture as your standard—the ruler against which you will measure all of your assumptions. Why? Because the Bible is the one source of truth from which all truth about your identity stems. However, if you question the accuracy and inerrancy of Scripture, you will have a difficult time embracing your true identity because you will remain skeptical that it is indeed true.

If you have questions about the Bible, I applaud you! I am always encouraged by the person who wants more than a simplistic answer, someone who wants to truly believe for themselves, not because someone else told them to. People with questions and doubts are people who refuse to be "fed a line" and are hungry for truth. As the Bible is the one book that a Christian bases his or her faith and life upon, it is paramount that you believe it. Those who do believe it is God's holy Word, timeless and without error, have sought answers to their difficult and challenging questions. In so doing, they become even more established in their faith than before.

Your questions about the accuracy, validity, or truth of the Bible are legitimate and deserve to be answered. It is simply not in the scope of this book to do so, as volumes of comprehensive sources have all ready been published on the subject. That's why I've compiled a list of recommended reading for you. (See appendix 3, "Recommended Reading.") The first step in excavating and correcting your faulty assumptions is to examine the beliefs you have about yourself through the lens of God's Word. (You've already written out some of those beliefs in your answers to the first four Questions for Reflection for this chapter.) Dig into the Bible with an eye for what it says about women. Read what Jesus says to specific women; discover how He interacts with them. (We will do this together in chapter 6). Dig into the four Gospels and put yourself in the stories with Jesus, imagining you are the woman with whom He is interacting. Let it become much more than words on a page. Let it become an experience. If you had this encounter with Jesus face-to-face, how would it affect who you think you are? Ask and allow God to change you through your reading.

As you examine the Bible, you will find that women can be looked to as role models (consider Ruth and Sarah in the Old Testament and Mary and Elizabeth in the New). Women are effective leaders, teachers, and evangelists (Lydia, Apphia, Nympha, Chloe, Priscilla, Dorcas, and the Samaritan woman at the well). Women are hard workers for the Lord (Tryphena, Tryphosa, Persis, Euodia, Syntyche, and Phoebe). And women have great value in God's sight (the woman hemorrhaging for twelve years, the "sinner" who anoints Christ's feet, Mary Magdalene, and more).

Dig into the Bible with an eye
for what it says about women.

Secondly, you must recognize your assumptions for what they are—your own. Without other perspectives, we easily become presumptuous, arrogant, and ignorant. "A fool finds no pleasure in understanding but delights in airing his own opinions" (Prov. 18:2). Think about the example of the young men learning the Lisu language. Realize that your opinion comes from only one angle—and it may be far from accurate. Be willing to turn the prism of your worldview, and make God the center of it. Boldly seek other perspectives and prepare to have your eyes opened!

Thirdly, as you seek a biblical perspective and listen to others, do so with a teachable spirit. Keep in mind that you will never "arrive"; you will never reach a point where you can quit learning. Seeking insight and growth is a process—the key word being *process*. Let your learning and growth continue indefinitely! Notice the present tense in Proverbs 18:15: "The heart of the discerning *acquires* knowledge; the ears of the wise *seek* it out" (emphasis mine). It does not say the discerning and wise are so because they *once* sought and acquired knowledge. Rather, they continue to pursue knowledge. They continue to learn. Strive first to understand before being understood, considering Proverbs 18:12–13, "Before his downfall a man's heart is proud, but humility comes before honor. He who answers before listening—that is his folly and his shame."

Finally, a word of warning ... this journey is not always an easy one. Make the commitment now that you will not give up when emotional issues arise and wounds open, tempting you to give up. Don't let inner reactions hinder your growth. Instead, let your good, bad, and ugly feelings, doubts, and insecurities spur you closer to God. He wants your healing more than you do. He's the One who wants you to believe His perspective—His truth!—more than anyone. Cling to Him in prayer, confessing that which hinders you and asking Him to free you from the assumptions you've made and the lies you believe.

Prayer

Lord, I recognize my faulty assumptions for what they are, and I confess I have let them blind me from Your truth. I have been living in a false reality because it is one not founded on Your truth. Please help me excavate my faulty assumptions. Give me endurance, along with strength and vulnerability to turn the corner in my life. Guide me faithfully and lovingly through this process, I pray. Amen.

Chapter 3

How the Picture Got Distorted

In the last chapter we looked at personal assumptions—beliefs we hold that we often don't even know we have. While personal history and self-knowledge are indeed important, to better understand the nature of our assumptions as they relate to our value as women, we must consider the bigger picture that exists beyond our individual life and immediate circumstances. Why? Because, as the saying goes, "No man is an island."

What this means is that no individual is so solitary that she (or he) is not influenced by others. The assumptions you hold about your value as a woman, about who you are, were not formed in a vacuum. You are a part of a much bigger world than your *self*. You are a part of a family, yes. A body of believers, yes. A neighborhood or local community, yes. Each of these influences in your life may seem like an easy target to blame for whatever misguided beliefs or assumptions have shaped you. But before playing the blame game, we must consider the whole picture.

As stated in chapter 1, a war is being waged against women today. A distorted view of woman is everywhere. It does not discriminate by class, beauty, health, culture, or religion … only gender. Women have been put down, lied to, mistreated, robbed of basic human rights, and stripped of their intrinsic worth for generations. In fact, this has happened throughout history!

In order to better understand our faulty assumptions about our value, we must consider history from the time God first created humankind. As we examine what happened in the past, and the influence of culture and philosophies, we begin to see how our views and values in the twenty-first century have been shaped. We were born into a history and world that continue unfolding today. So let's look at how our lives fit into this intricate story.

How It All Began

Our view of ourselves—our self-image, who we think are—and our sense of value have been tarnished and corrupted since mankind first fell into sin. Here's a brief biblical account of how it all unfolded: God created man and woman in His own image (Gen. 1:27). Adam was the first man, Eve was the first woman. God blessed them, telling them to be fruitful and increase in number. Both male and female were created by God to bear His image (Gen. 1:26–28).

> Consider with me how cultures, peoples, and religions have been twisting the truth about women since the time of Adam and Eve.

Eve listened to the serpent who told her she would become like God, knowing good from evil, if she ate the fruit of the tree of the knowledge of good and evil (Gen. 2:16–17; 3:1–5). She ate the fruit that God had forbidden them to eat. Adam listened to Eve, and he ate the fruit too. Both fell into sin. Adam and Eve "hid" from God, and shame entered the picture. But God sought them out. Then Adam blamed Eve, Eve blamed the serpent, and God blamed them all (Gen. 3:6–19). *Much of the world has been blaming Eve and, by extension, devaluing women ever since.*

A language professor at a Middle Eastern seminary sat in on a class I taught in Jordan one summer not too long ago. He was well educated and able to teach and speak in Chinese, English, and

Arabic. He told me that woman had to be kept under control of man because she's not to be trusted. After all, she's the one who led him into sin. His theory that women are more easily tempted and not fit to be trusted is one that many people simply accept as true. A negative view of women from the beginning, blaming them for humanity's fall into sin, persists to this day.

Scripture makes it clear that shame is one of the consequences all of humankind experiences as a result of the fall. And some of us were taught to be ashamed just because we are female. Keeping in mind the biblical account of creation and the fall (Gen. 1–3), consider with me how cultures, peoples, and religions have been twisting the truth about women since the time of Adam and Eve.

Were They Always Great Thinkers?

Teaching a false, corrupt view of women has deep roots in religious, cultural, and societal history. Since the beginning of early civilization in most pagan, Roman, Greek, Jewish, and Islamic cultures, thinking toward women has been negative. To put it mildly, women were cast in a bad light. They were seen primarily as objects of pleasure, instruments for procreation, or temptresses who lead men into sin. "Poets, philosophers and physicians from Homer (eighth century BC) to Galen (first century AD) speak with remarkable consistency of woman as object … [believing] women are passive and even the best of them are inferior to men."[1]

Many of the earliest of our world's cultures practiced the subjugation and denigration of women. In fact, life was so undesirable that mothers even thought about exterminating their newborn daughters to save them the heartache of growing up female. "Everywhere the life of a woman was considered cheaper than that of a man; and when girls were born there was none of the rejoicing that marked the coming of a male. Mothers sometimes destroyed their female children to keep them from misery."[2] Of course, not all men and women in these early cultures thought of women in this way, but the view was common and acceptable. And, unfortunately, many of those whose thoughts were consistent with these beliefs wrote about them.

Having found their way onto papyrus, these ideas heavily influenced the early Greek and Roman thinking that is foundational to Western culture today, not to mention Judaism and Christianity. None of us are immune from having our thinking influenced by the world around us. The culture we live in and the philosophies that circulate in our world shape us. What we don't realize is that the great thinkers of each historical time period were also influenced by the attitudes of the day. That includes those men who laid the foundation for belief systems that still exist in one form or another. Consider the great philosophers who so impacted the world that they continue to be taught in Western colleges and universities today. Socrates (469–399 BC), who predates Plato and Aristotle, often referred to women as the weaker sex, and "argued that being born a woman is a divine punishment, since a woman is halfway between a man and an animal."[3]

Plato (427–347 BC) introduced the theory of dualism, the idea that for every one thing in the cosmos, there is an equal and opposite other. "This theory had a profound impact on the way that women were viewed, and it was not to women's advantage. 'Woman' was placed in a category containing elements that were viewed as negative. They were seen as closer to the natural/animal world than men. By nature they were irrational and untrustworthy, and therefore unfit to make their own decisions and govern their own lives. They had to be looked after and controlled, never treated as equals."[4] Does that mindset, prevalent before the time of Christ, sound a little like the professor I met in Jordan more than two thousand years later?

Also consider that Aristotle (384–322 BC), "for his part, held that women are systematically inferior to men in every respect—anatomically, physiologically, and ethically—and that this inferiority is a consequence of their metaphysical passivity. Great men said terrible things about women. Great philosophies and respected sciences established false and contemptuous ideas about the feminine."[5] For all the progressive thinking Aristotle contributed, his firm belief in sexual discrimination was a huge step backward for everyone then *and* now.

Cultures and Society

Women were seen as objects—created to be used by men. If you are an object, then it follows that you can be bought or sold for a price. That is just what happened to women in so many of the cultures prior to the time of Christ. They were viewed as chattel to be bought and sold. What do you think this attitude toward women communicated to her about her eternal value? Do you think that these historical beliefs could have been passed down as generational sin, assaulting our minds today?

> The great thinkers of each historical time period were also influenced by the attitudes of the day.

In the ancient Greek culture around 1300–1100 BC, husbands were free to beat their wives, as there was no law against it. Concubines (a woman who lives with a man but is not married to him) were common among men who could afford a large household.[6] A quote from Pseudo-Demosthenes (340 BC) summarizes the lives of women in antiquity: "Mistresses we keep for the sake of pleasure, concubines for the daily care of our person, but wives to bear us legitimate children to be faithful guardians of our households."[7] Such was the case then and into the eighteenth century in Europe, and even still in many cultures around the world today. Consider the weight that individual women are bearing on their shoulders today from thousands of years of history of women being consistently devalued. It influences her understanding of who she is as a woman.

What of early Roman culture? "Birth itself was an adventure in Rome. If the child was deformed or female, the father was permitted by custom to expose it to death."[8] Woman enjoyed a bit higher status (if she lived!), but there was no such thing as "created equal in God's image." Do you think this is not an issue for women in our world today? Guess again. As recently as forty years ago, infanticide of children who were sickly or female was practiced in the Masaai culture in Africa. Though this horrible practice is against the law now in Kenya and Tanzania, it still occurs in some outlying regions.

Turning to another influence that is powerful in our world today, we find that from the earliest days of the Islam religion, women were scorned. Not surprisingly, the same was true of the culture surrounding the founder of Islam, the prophet Muhammad (570–632). In pre-Islamic Arabia, men could marry as many as ten wives at a time. In addition, "a husband could have a mistress and the wife a lover without any restrictions. Incest was practiced, with fathers marrying their daughters. A son was allowed to marry his stepmother after the death of his father. A man could divorce his wife just by saying the words of dismissal 'go whenever you want,' and she had no redress to law. A woman was an object to be inherited like money, but she could inherit nothing from her husband or her son."[9]

Devout Muslims will defend Muhammad, saying he valued women. They quote a well-known statement of his that "the best among you is he who is good to his family."[10] However, the Koran also specifically mentions that a husband is allowed to beat his wife if he feels her behavior is rebellious.[11] We know that Muhammad had many wives (most sources say twelve), and he had relations with concubines and slaves as well.

Inconsistencies and controversies are many regarding a woman's value in Islamic culture. But it is safe to say that in most Islamic countries, she is and has always been subservient to man, lacking many personal rights. These cultural norms communicate that she lacks personal value, that she is of no worth. Phil Parshall states, "Fundamentalist Islam has contributed to the oppression and pain of millions of Muslim women worldwide."[12]

In Jordan, Islam is the religion of the country and is claimed by more than 80 percent of the population. In 2006, a woman from Jordan shared with me a bit of her story.

> My name is Um Sarah. I used to always hear how a woman will end up in hell as it was mentioned in Hadith, where he [Muhammad] says, "I looked in hell and I saw women were in the majority and I looked in heaven and the poor were the majority"

> (Al Bukhari, Nukaa 87).[13] And also, he says that whatever the woman does, she is always the source of pessimism, for "the pessimism in three: a woman, a female horse, and the house" (Al Bukhari, Jihad 47).[14]
>
> I used to always wonder why all troubles go hand in hand with women. I used to feel that for some reason God doesn't love girls or women, so why then did He create us? So He can enjoy our torture? Then later on I learned that a woman was created only to please the man, and if she doesn't listen to her man's call to please him, she will be cursed by all the angels—as if the angels have nothing to do but to curse us. Also, Hadith says, "When a man calls his wife to sleep with him and she refuses, he goes to bed angry and the angels curse her until morning" (Al Bukhari Bida al khalk 7, Nukka 15).[15] All these supposedly holy sayings made me feel rejected for just being human, for just being a woman.

A Christian friend of mine told me about an experience she had recently with Fadua, a woman in Morocco, which is also a Muslim country. My friend asked Fadua what she thought about Jesus. She responded, "I do not think anything. I do not know—that is something for men."

My friend explained to me, "For her and other women in her area, believing and thinking are things that men do. Their only purpose in life is to be married, bear children, and take care of the house. That's it. They are not taken into account as people. It does not matter what they feel or think. It is as if they have no soul."

Please don't misunderstand me here. I highly value the roles of wife, mother, and homemaker. But these roles, even fulfilled to perfection, will not get you into heaven, *nor* are they the reasons women are highly valued by God. He values us because of *who* we *are*, not because of *what* we *do*.

Jewish Culture in Biblical Times

Jewish rabbinical thought often mirrored Greek thought. Rabbinical leaders taught that women were uneducable. Women were also considered by many conservative rabbis to be unreliable courtroom witnesses, and they were held responsible for the lustful temptations of men.

In ancient Israel women lived in a patriarchal culture. A woman was an "asset" of her husband, but she could not be sold. Girls married shortly after puberty, participated in the economic tasks of the household, and were given the primary social role of bearing children. A married woman with children had a certain place of honor, but even that position was tied to her ability to have sons.

A woman was supposed to be respected; after all, a good Jew living around 500 BC and later would try to obey the Ten Commandments that state very clearly, "Honor your father *and* your mother" (Ex. 20:12, emphasis mine). But her value was largely found in her ability to produce male heirs. Even today, when a wife gives birth to a girl, they say *kafa,* Arabic for "that's enough." It is still prevalent; I learned the saying recently on a trip to the Middle East. Sons remain much more preferred than daughters. This mindset reflects the ancient words of Ben Sira written around 180–175 BC: "It is a disgrace to be the father of an undisciplined son, and the birth of a daughter is a loss."[16] At that time it was crucial for a woman's sense of value and identity to produce male heirs to inherit property, work the land or a trade, and hold positions of leadership in the community.

> He values us because of *who* we are, not because of *what* we do.

Can you see how this belief is perhaps "inherited thinking," a result of generational sin?

In Jewish life, a woman's sphere of influence was limited almost exclusively to her family. She lived in an agrarian culture where her husband worked the land or a trade near or at home. He was "on site," so to speak, and usually ate the midday meal with the family. When children were old enough, they learned to work alongside their fathers and mothers. The family then spent much more time together than they do in our modern world.

However, family laws were weighted in favor of men. "The laws of inheritance, betrothal, and divorce were heavily biased in the male's favor, with only a few checks and balances."[17] A woman could institute a divorce against her husband for a divorce price, but it was frowned upon and possible only under difficult circumstances. She was passed to husband from father, normally with little or no concern for what she wanted or thought. At puberty, around age twelve or thirteen, a girl could be betrothed by her father and informed as to whom she would marry. This practice continues in many cultures today.

Jewish women were allowed to publicly participate in some religious observances. However, most were practiced at home rather than in the public assembly. In time, rabbinical writings expanded their interpretation of the Old Testament laws and how they were to be lived out. Woman's roles in the worshipping community became increasingly restricted through rules written by men that God never designed.

This was the cultural scene into which Jesus Christ was born. But Christ did not follow society's norms. His behavior was radically countercultural and flew in the face of Jewish customs. Through His words and actions, He accorded women new life and dignity. We will examine how He did so, and the significance and value He intentionally brings to you as a woman, in chapter 6. Right now, let's examine the impact of the Christian church.

The New Testament Era and the New Church

Just after the time of Christ, in the first days and years of the Christian faith, women were coming to know their Savior, and they were on fire for Him! Historians will tell you that early Christianity was the religion of slaves, the poor, and women. Why do you think that was? Given the historical, cultural, and societal setting just described, you can see how the disenfranchised would naturally be attracted to Him. Jesus was a man who communicated respect and value, something not being offered by anyone else.

Women were some of the great early evangelists! They shared their faith and engaged in ministry. Consider the work, effort, and lives of Priscilla (wife of Aquila), Junias, Phoebe, Tryphena and Tryphosa, Persis, Nympha, Lydia, Dorcas, Mary, and Elizabeth. Women were received by Christ as disciples, as ones who could learn, sit at His feet, and serve alongside Him. This was new freedom for them, and they embraced it. Men and women colabored together for the advancement of the Gospel. (See Luke 10:38–42 and Acts 18.)

During the first 100–150 years after Christ, women were prominent in the church as it was developing. The early Christian community met in homes. These communities, as illustrated in Acts 2:42–44, had everything in common. They knew each other intimately and shared all they had with each other. Women opened their homes, extended hospitality, and gave of their time, energy, and resources.

But as the church grew, and as believers sought to live out the principles of faith and human value as taught by Christ, they remained heavily influenced by Jewish and pagan beliefs that diminished women.

> Within a few short centuries of Jesus' lifetime, theologians were arguing that the female soul is as different from the male's as the female body is from the male's. In 584, for example, at the Council of Macon in Lyons, France, the nature of woman's humanity was debated by the elders of the church. The debate asked, "Do women have souls?" What was at issue was whether or not women should be considered as human or as something less than human. Ultimately the church fathers determined that indeed women did have souls and were therefore human. The issue was decided, however, by only one vote. [18]

By 700–1300 AD, "[T]he theories of churchmen were generally hostile to woman; some laws of the Church enhanced her subjection."[19] The church fathers advocated a life of seclusion and encouraged her to refrain from involvement in anything that took her out of the home. And though some "principles and practices of Christianity improved her status ... [T]o priests and theologians, woman was still in these centuries what she had seemed to Chrysostom: 'A necessary evil, a natural temptation, a desirable calamity, a domestic peril, a deadly fascination, a painted ill.'"[20]

Remember, secular thinking and much early Church thinking positioned woman as the wicked, weak temptress. The Church fathers were influenced by the dualistic thinking taught by Plato that women were less than men. The common thought was to protect her from irrationally falling prey to Satan's tricks. "Traditional Christian theology theoretically viewed all humanity as equally impaired by original sin, but in practice women were more impaired because it was their nature to be less logical and less rational. Woman's deprivation because of sin was therefore equated with depravity, and many church fathers echoed the teaching of Tertullian, who stressed that man should beware of woman—for she is the devil's gateway."[21]

However, if a woman modeled herself after the revered Virgin Mary by remaining virginal and wholly dedicated, often literally "married" to God, then she might become highly regarded. There was no middle ground. Until the Protestant Reformation in the sixteenth century, women were generally not wholly valued or fully embraced as God's image bearers.

> Jesus was a man who communicated respect and value, something not being offered by anyone else.

Martin Luther (1483–1546) examined the teachings and assumptions of the Catholic Church in his day, with results that were of course revolutionary. Among the many principles he challenged was traditional dualism. Instead he correctly preached the priesthood of all believers: that men and women are one in Christ and have a Kingdom role to play (1 Pet. 2:9). He also taught a higher view of the sanctity of marriage, rejecting the distinction between the "inferior" life of marriage vs. the "higher" religious world of the virginal monk and nun. Though the Catholic Church at this time regarded marriage as a sacrament, it taught that celibacy was preferable and that marriage was only designed for procreation and as a solution for human lust. But Luther and other Reformers believed that marriage was more than that: it was something that God had Himself commanded in Genesis 1:28 and 2:23–24; it was good and holy (not a sacrament, but sacred, an important distinction); and it was to reflect the highest love known to humans, the love of God. Woman's role in the home as wife and mother was now elevated—it was a calling of God. This role elevation resulted in an improved view of women. By turning to Scripture as his guide, Luther brought a much-needed dose of truth to the church's attitude toward women.

From the Protestant Reformation onward, there continued to be course corrections in the church's view of women. As the Protestant arm of the church grew in its understanding of the priesthood of all believers, women were increasingly grabbing hold of a more biblical view of who they were: significant, loved individuals with unique purpose. And the result was more women were embracing the truth.

For about two thousand years, there has been great tension between the freedom that Christ taught and the changing societal norms of the day and culture. Of course, some men (like Luke, the author of Luke and Acts) have recognized Christ's teaching and in turn respected and honored women. Other men, including many of those in church leadership, clung to a theology that was dishonoring to women. Theirs was not a wholly Christian worldview; rather, it was a blend of pagan and Christian thinking.

That Brings Us to Today

Conflicting views about women perpetuate the debate in the Christian church today. Much of the discord is motivated by blameless intentions—men and women wanting to honor God by accurately interpreting Scripture. It is more common today, at least in America, to find both sexes agreeing that God created both men and women in His image and with equal value (Gen. 1:27). But the debate about their appropriate roles in marriage and in church ministry continues.

Confusion regarding women's roles and value in the Body of Christ has persisted since the time of Christ. The fact that such a debate exists at all helps cast a negative light on the value and biblical identity of a woman.

The information in this chapter is not meant to discourage you, though the historical and cultural realities into which we were born are hardly uplifting. It's meant to help you by highlighting the reality that you are indeed not an island. The sin of disrespecting women has been with us since the Garden of Eden, and it is a worldwide problem. The devaluation of woman has been passed down to us from the beginning of time. How could it *not* affect who we think we are? It's easy to see how our grandparents, parents, and now *we* have inherited a predisposition to regard women—and to see ourselves—as "less than." With her dignity and worth continually questioned since the beginning of time, women today, Christian and non-Christian alike, often accept and respond to the lies by failing to live out their holy destiny as designed by God.

You may think it impossible to have any other view of women, including yourself, than that which has been passed down through the ages. To do otherwise may make you feel like you're swimming upstream. But I encourage you—do not give up before you even begin! I'm writing so passionately to you because the perspective that has been passed down to you through the ages is a lie. It's time to reject it! The distorted and corrupt picture of woman does not reflect you. It does not define you. It is not your true identity. I will state this truth again and again, because for us to even begin to accept it, we need to be told it again and again.

With this, we are ready to move away from examining the corrupt view of woman and into the liberating truth!

Prayer

God, here I am—just one woman living in the twenty-first century, born into a world that has attacked the value of a woman for thousands of years. I confess the bitterness I have harbored against those in my life, as well as those throughout world history, who have played a part in my inaccurate estimation of myself as a woman. I want to move into Your truth now with an open mind and heart. Guide me as we go. Amen.

Part Two

Truth from the Triune God

In the first three chapters of this book we examined the problem: Women, even Christian women, are not living the truth about their true value and identity. Too often we have allowed our sense of worth, our belief about who we are, to be determined by faulty assumptions, societal and cultural norms, our personal experiences, erroneous and sinful thought patterns, family members, the media, and even Satan himself. Is our value (and identity) to be found in our roles (as mother, wife, career woman, etc.), our gender, our looks, our smarts, or anything else? Or is our true identity, an identity that has immeasurable value, found in something else?

Let's unearth the answer
you've been seeking …

Christian or not, women the whole world over are often confused and misinformed. The truth of our value and identity has been so skewed that it's virtually unrecognizable among the lies. A cosmic mind change is needed in cultures and societies around the world. But it won't happen on a grand scale if it doesn't first happen on an individual level. Nothing will change unless *you* allow a change to happen in *you*.

The next four chapters make up the second part of this book. They unveil the simple, beautiful, profound truth. They describe in detail the answer you've been longing for, but perhaps have been misunderstanding or missing altogether. The truth—the answer!—is simple. It is found in knowing the one true personal, relational, triune God. It is found in the entire Godhead: God the Father, Jesus the Son, and the Holy Spirit. These three communicate a unified message of your value, extraordinary design, and significance as a woman.

But, you may protest, *I know God! That's why I'm reading this book. I'm a Christian; I do know Jesus Christ as my Lord and Savior. Though I have accepted that He did die for me, I still don't feel worthwhile.*

Logically, you get it. You know that God has placed His stamp of approval on women and on you specifically. It's getting this truth from your head to your heart that's posing a problem. It is moving the truth from an intellectual nod of the head to a life-changing experience. No one can do that but *you,* in cooperation with the Holy Spirit.

For others, this may involve encountering Christ for the first time, like the woman at the well in John 4, and having a soul-redeeming, transformational experience. And this too, is a deeply personal event. As we move into this next part, my prayer is not that you find a new answer to the question of your worth (because the answer hasn't changed; it will always be found in God), but that you will find a new, more richly multifaceted perspective on God and His truth than you could ever imagine. And that will be your key to grasping and living out your incomparable worth.

You may be accustomed to relating with God as simply God. Or, a little more personally, you might see Him as your Father. Others keep Him at arm's length and see Him as "Master." In any case, when you fail to grasp the reality of the *triune* God, the God that coexists perfectly together as Father, Son, and Holy Spirit yet is One, you miss out on, well, the reality of a many-sided God! Why is this important? Because God has revealed more of Himself than just Father or Master. Each Person of the Trinity answers one of your three core needs as a woman. He knows who you are. And the Trinity presents a unified message of your significance and value. He tells us this truth; it is up to us to accept it.

Let's go! Let's unearth the answer you've been seeking …

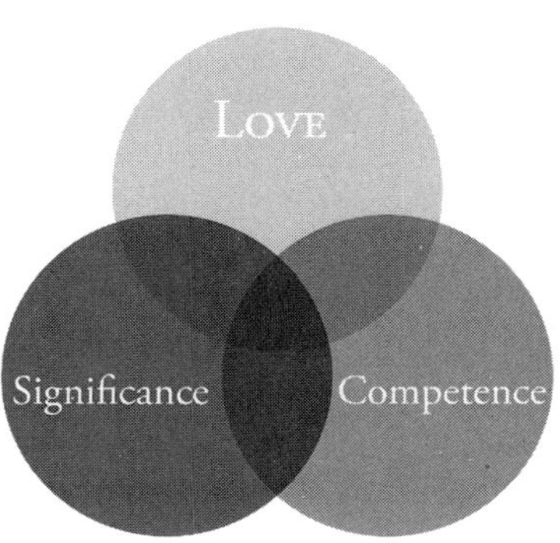

Chapter 4

Created by the Father

You want to feel loved. More than that, you need to. The need to feel valuable, loved, and worthwhile is universal among human beings. Psychologists say that love is one of our three core needs, and that everyone aspires to feel good about themselves. Part of feeling worthwhile comes from the experience of being loved.

To that end, I have good news: *You, woman, have been created with love by God the Father.* It's a simple truth. So simple, it's easy to miss its profound impact. Read it again, only this time put yourself in the sentence, and pause to ponder the different areas of emphasis:

- *I* (your name), am a woman
- who has been *created*
- with *love*
- by God the *Father.*

The first part—*you*—is not difficult to grasp. You know yourself. You have, after all, been living with your own company your entire life. You know what you like, what you dislike, how you think, feel, and live. You are quite familiar with your ways. But strip away your exterior actions and even your internal motivations—who are you at your core?

In order to answer that question, in order to understand who we are and become established in our true identity, we must first recognize what we are *not*. We are not defined by what happens to us. Someone who survives a rape cannot be reduced to being simply a "rape survivor." We are not defined by our physical features.

Someone who has had her leg amputated cannot be reduced to being simply "an amputee." We are not what we do. The CEO of a company cannot be reduced to being simply "a successful career woman."

To understand who we are at our core, we have to start with God. Because God created us, our identity is rooted in Him alone. And that identity is rooted in God as manifested in His triune nature—Father, Son, and Holy Spirit.

To understand the reality that you have been created with love by God the Father, let's dive into and expand upon the sentence as broken down in the bullet points above. We'll examine the last three bullet points in this chapter. We'll consider the first bullet point—what it means that you are created uniquely *woman*—in further depth in the next chapter.

You Are *Created*

You are a created being. You didn't "just happen." Not only did you not "just happen," you were also not created "just because." You are not an evolutionary accident or a mistake of nature. The truth is that you were created with a purpose. That can be hard to see on an everyday basis, with chores to keep up, relationships to maintain, and jobs to get done. But your purpose is much more splendid, and if you fail to identify it, your daily life will feel empty and meaningless.

What is your purpose? It is to bear God's image, and to bring Him glory by loving Him, living for Him, and reflecting Him in and through your life. It really is that plain and simple. Considering that God is almighty and all powerful, this is a high calling. From the beginning, this has been God's design for you.

Genesis, the first book in the Bible, starts at the beginning of time. It's the creation account. We see here how God formed everything we know: time, the earth, the animals, and mankind. Nothing around us is unaccounted for. "Then God said, 'Let us make man in our image, in our likeness, and let them rule over the fish of the sea and the birds of the air, over the livestock, over all the earth, and over all the creatures that move along the ground.' So God created man in his own image, in the image of God he created him; male and female he created them" (Gen. 1:26–27).

There it is, plain as day. This passage is describing the profound truth that we humans are created by God. We didn't magically appear, we didn't scientifically combust, and we didn't evolve from something else. We were created. We are *creatures*. Along with the animals on land and in the air and sea, we are intentionally created beings.

In and of itself, this is an astounding fact! What's more, we are unique and set apart from every other living being because we are created *in God's image*. Nothing else that has breath bears the image of God—only humans do. And that includes both men and women.

If you think men are even slightly superior, bearing God's image more accurately than women, you are deceived. Both genders are equally endowed with this honor. "This is the written account of Adam's line. When God created man, he made him in the likeness of God. He created them male and female and blessed them. And when they were created, he called them 'man'" (Gen. 5:1–2).

With the arrival of the first offspring, we also see that not only Adam and Eve, but every generation that follows in turn bears God's image. "When Adam had lived 130 years, he had a son in his own likeness, in his own image; and he named him Seth" (Gen. 5:3). God is the Father of Adam. Adam is the father of Seth. Our status as image bearers has been passed on from generation to generation. But God the Father is Father of us all.

Like a copy is the exact representation of an original, so too do children bear God's image as precisely as did Adam and Eve. When humans reproduce, children are not "copies of copies" that diminish the accuracy of the original image of God; they bear God's image exactly. That means that you bear God's image just as significantly today as the first man and woman did ages ago.

> Your purpose is to bear God's image and to bring Him glory by loving Him, living for Him, and reflecting Him in your life.

Again in Genesis chapter 9 we are told, "For in the image of God has God made man" (Gen. 9:6). This truth is evident throughout Scripture. We cannot deny our high calling. But how can it mean anything to us if we do not know we are made in the image of God?

Often when we hear the word *image,* we think of a picture—something we can see. Many of us give up trying to understand the image of God because we cannot see Him physically. But an image is much more than physical features for the eyes to see. An image is a total picture to be grasped with our mind, intellect, spirit, emotions, and soul … our entire being. And there is much about God's image to be gleaned from Scripture.

Created like *God ...*

The two phrases "in our image" and "in our likeness" (Gen. 1:26) are very similar in the original Hebrew language. We represent God—that's "image." And we are like God—that's "likeness." The bottom line is that men and women are representations of God. We are patterned after Him. We are like Him in certain respects. Our intrinsic value is rooted in this fact.

How specifically are we like Him? Scripture again gives us some answers.

We are like God in our calling to rule over creation. "God blessed them and said to them, 'Be fruitful and increase in number; fill the earth and subdue it. Rule over the fish of the sea and the birds of the air and over every living creature that moves on the ground'" (Gen. 1:28). God rules His universe (Ps. 103:19), and He has instructed us to rule and subdue the earth. He has given us this responsibility, and, as we observe the world around us, we see that mankind has certainly responded by doing just that throughout time.

We are also like God in that we are relational beings. Read all of Genesis 1 and note the phrase "let us." It is first used in Genesis 1:26 when God is creating man and woman. This is the first evidence of God's triune nature. God does not say, "Let *me*." He says, "Let *us*" because He is the Trinity. He is three Persons in One.

The fundamental truth of one harmonious being composed of three distinct parts is that each of the three must be in a cohesive relationship with the others. (Imagine three people in a boat, each trying to paddle it in a different direction. The boat wouldn't go anywhere but perhaps in circles. Struggle, strife, and futility would punctuate such an entity.) The essence of the Trinity is a sweet relationship between each of the three Persons: Father, Son, and Holy Spirit. Each is in agreement with the others.

Because God's very nature is relational and we are made in His image, we also are relational beings. We reflect Him as He exists in three Persons. He is not alone. He wants us to be in relationship with Him (all three Persons of the Trinity), as well as with one another. Relationship is very important to God.

Human life is sacred because each and every person is an image bearer of God.

Before God made Eve, Adam was struggling on his own. God recognized his need for fellowship. "So the LORD God caused the man to fall into a deep sleep; and while he was sleeping, he took one of the man's ribs and closed up the place with flesh. Then the LORD God made a woman from the rib he had taken out of the man, and he brought her to the man" (Gen. 2:21–22).

Clearly, fellowship is a priority for God. He designed us as social beings as well, and built that need into us. We are also thinking, feeling, and choosing beings with identity and personality, and so is our Creator.[1]

… *And* unlike *God*

While it is important to note the ways we are like God—and these are just a few—it is equally important to note the ways in which we are unlike God. Scripture is clear that we are made *in God's image*, not *as* God, little gods, or equal to God. We are not His clones, nor his robots. And we are certainly not His equal.

The secular mindset popular in America today asserts, "We are all gods." It promotes focus and dedication to the trinity of self-absorption: me, myself, and I. This isn't exactly the correct Trinity whom we are created to worship! It's a perspective that removes God from His throne and promotes worshipping "the god within"—idolizing ourselves over God.

This kind of thinking mistakenly puts man in God's place. The truth is that we are independent beings. God gives us choice. Everyone has the God-given freedom to choose. We make decisions by our own will, and we decide whether we will accept God in our lives as our heavenly Father, or whether we will turn to gods of our own making (Josh. 24:15).

God will always be greater than humankind. As our study of the creation account begins in the first book of the Bible, note what God says about Himself in the last book in the Bible: "I am the Alpha and the Omega, the First and the Last, the Beginning and the End" (Rev. 22:13). He alone is perfect, holy, just, and true. The Creator is always greater than the created. All the pages in between the first and last books of the Bible are packed with evidence supporting this truth.

"Shall what is formed say to him who formed it, 'He did not make me'? Can the pot say of the potter, 'He knows nothing'?" (Isa. 29:16). God the Father is to be revered as Creator. Man is but His creation. "The builder of a house has greater honor than the house itself. For every house is built by someone, but God is the builder of everything" (Heb. 3:3–4). We owe our every breath to Him, "for in him we live and move and have our being" (Acts 17:28).

Another distinguishing factor between mankind and God is that while we are made in a woman's womb, God the Father is self-existent and eternal. He was not made in a mother's womb. We are finite; He is eternal. The psalmist reminds us we are not made of a man and woman's decision, but by God: "For you created my inmost being; you knit me together in my mother's womb. I praise you because I am fearfully and wonderfully made; your works are wonderful, I know that full well" (Ps. 139:13–14).

We also know that God is above, and we are below. Psalm 8:4–6 says, "What is man that you are mindful of him, the son of man that you care for him? You made him a little lower than the heavenly beings and crowned him with glory and honor. You made him ruler over the works of your hands; you put everything under his feet." As awesome as the responsibility is that He has given us to rule over *His* creation, by no stretch of the imagination can we ever elevate ourselves to His heights in the heavenly realm.

The image is tarnished yet enduring.

While man is made in God's image, note that Adam and Eve's disobedience in the Garden stained this image of God. The image of God was no longer perfectly expressed through man. Sin marred it. Death then became a part of life. It has been for as long as we have known, but God never originally intended life to end with death. Still, we see the slaying of the first animal was done by God Himself. *When* did God do this? After Adam and Eve disobeyed. *Why* did God do this? To provide tunics of animal skin for them because they were ashamed of their nakedness (Gen. 3:6–11, 21). This is an amazing picture of His love for us, that He continued to love us and meet our needs even after our disobedience.

Soon after this, the first murder occurs when Cain kills his brother Abel (Gen. 4). Evil and wickedness abound to the point that God floods the earth, saving only those few pleasing to Him, Noah and his family (Gen. 6–7).

With a new start, God tells man, "Everything that lives and moves will be food for you. Just as I gave you the green plants, I now give you everything" (Gen. 9:3). But human life remains sacred. He says, "And from each man, too, I will demand an accounting for the life of his fellow man. Whoever sheds the blood of man, by man shall his blood be shed; for in the image of God has God made man" (Gen. 9:5–6).

Though we have tarnished it, God's unique and holy image remains the core of our identity. Because we bear God's image, our lives are sacred, valuable, and prized above all the rest of creation. Human life is sacred because each and every person is an image bearer of God.

Anthony Hoekema says, "[W]hen one kills a human being, not only does he take that person's life, but he hurts God himself—the God who was reflected in that individual. To touch the image of God is to touch God himself; to kill the image of God is to do violence to God himself."[2] This foundational truth is at the heart of the Christian's (and God's) abhorrence of violent acts toward humanity. Any attack on one of God's image bearers strikes at not only the person, but also the image of God within her! This includes wife abuse, child abuse, murder … even self-abuse.

If our understanding of what it means to be created in God's image is vague, skewed, or obstructed altogether, we will never accurately live our true identity. Our tendency will be toward self-denigration or outright self-hatred. Our challenge is to see ourselves as we truly are: created persons, God's image bearers, a little lower than the heavenly beings, crowned with glory and honor (Ps. 8:5), with life that is consecrated and gifted for an eternal purpose. It's true: Your intrinsic value is rooted in the fact that you are patterned after the almighty God Himself.

You Are Created with *Love*

You, woman, are created as God's image bearer. Let this fact sink in over the next several days. Hold it gently and admire it from every angle, as you might a gift you have always wanted and just received. And brace yourself for even more. If being created for the purpose of reflecting Him to the world around you is not staggering enough, it gets better. The truth is you weren't created in a cold, sterile void like a mathematical equation producing a sum; you were created with *love*.

Love was never intended to be a luxury experienced by a select, elite few who deserve it. Quite the contrary; God communicates love to us *all* as both the majestic Father of all creation and as our personal, heavenly Father. The very act of His creating you and me is a message of love. God didn't *have* to create you. He *wanted* to. And He did not have to create you in His image. He *wanted* to. And He did not have to communicate these truths to you. He *wanted* to.

We live in a world where contractual agreements are the norm. We're used to people doing things because they are obligated to, not because they are motivated by their hearts. But love is not love when it is forced. And God was certainly not forced to create you or let you bear His image.

Just think—your core need for love is already met. It was met in the beginning! Before your physical body was created, God the Father was planning how to mold you, shape you, form and create you. This creation process in and of itself is an act of love. He poured His energy, creativity, and ingenuity into you. Your need for love and value was met in the very act of creation.

And now that He has brought you—mind, body, and soul—into existence, He's not done with you. He did not create you for the mere sake of creating. Now that you are alive, He wants to spend time with you! His love continues. He pursues you every day.

> Love was never intended to be a luxury experienced by a select, elite few who deserve it.

The love of Christ, the love of God

When Christians think of the "love of God," we often think of Jesus Christ. We envision His interactions, His words, His life, and ultimately His sacrifice of love for us on the cross. We somehow separate the love of Christ from the love of God. But God the Father has been displaying His love for us since the beginning of time. You find these displays throughout the Old and New Testaments.

Consider God in the beginning. When Adam and Eve sinned, they deliberately disobeyed God's one specific command about what *not* to do. How did God react to their disobedience? He could have annihilated them! It would have made perfect sense to have done so. He had every right to do so. He is just and righteous. Instead, He sought them out. He pursued them. And then He clothed them because they felt ashamed about their nakedness (which wasn't the case before they sinned). Did He have to do any of it? No. But He loved them, and He didn't want to give up on them. Now, millenniums later, He continues to seek you out.

It's not that God loved Adam and Eve so much that He ignored their sin. He most certainly did not. Any sin is an affront to God. Sin and holiness cannot coexist. Because God is just, there were consequences for Adam and Eve's sin just as there are consequences for each of us. What He did do was an astounding act of justice, love, and mercy. God the Father sent His Son, Jesus Christ, to pay the penalty for their sin (Rom. 3:25–26). And not for theirs alone—for ours, too.

"God demonstrates his own love for us in this: While we were still sinners, Christ died for us" (Rom. 5:8). Notice the two parts of the sentence. It's not that Christ died for us because only *He* loved us (as often in our minds we separate God's love from Christ's); it's that Christ died for us as a demonstration of *God's love.* We cannot have one without the other. We cannot have the love of God without Christ's death on the cross. And we cannot have Christ's death without God's love.

That means when you are having your absolute worst day or span of days, when you are the most ugly and ungodly person, Christ's sacrifice for you is enough to bring you back to right standing with God the Father. Our God loves to the extreme. It is not because He is obligated to or because we deserve it, but because that is who He is. God is love (1 John 4:8, 16). And He is passionate about you!

God's hesed *love*

The Hebrew word *hesed* describes God's love. The definition describes an active, selfless, sacrificial, devoted, caring love. "It's the way God intended for human beings to live together from the beginning. The 'love your neighbor as yourself' brand of living, an active, selfless, sacrificial caring for one another that goes against the grain of our fallen natures."[3]

There are two parties involved in this kind of love. The first party is someone in desperate need (you and me). The second is someone who possesses the power and resources to make a difference (God). Again, this love is driven not by duty or obligation, but by a bone-deep commitment; it is a loyal, selfless love that motivates a person to do voluntarily what no one has a right to expect or ask of him.

Now, get this: "[W]e were created to live in God's *hesed* love—to dwell in His love and thrive on His care. Having God's *hesed* is the best thing that could ever happen to anyone."[4] Oh, how we need to absorb, drink in, and wallow in this truth. He made us to live in His love—to want it and need it and grip it! We were created to live *in* God's love, not with mere head knowledge *about* God's love. God the Father's love is personal, glorious, perfect, infinite, and unchanging. This is the very love that brought you into existence. This is the very love with which God continues pursuing you today!

You Are Created with Love by God the *Father*

So who is this loving Father? Our heavenly Father is the first Person in the Trinity. The mystery of the Trinity is just that: a mystery. But the Bible is clear that though God is one being in essence, one divine nature, He is manifested in three Persons. We see the fullest expression of the Trinity in the New Testament, though there is evidence of the Trinity in the Old Testament (Gen. 1:2, 26; Isa. 63:10). As a united Godhead, the Father, Son, and Holy Spirit were all present at and had a part in Creation (Gen 1:26; John 1:1; Col.1:13–16), though the Father is generally referred to as our Creator. The Father is our "originator." All things come from the Father. He lovingly decreed that salvation would come to us through the Son Jesus Christ, who is "the image of the invisible God, the firstborn over all creation" (Col.1:15–16), and He sent the Holy Spirit to make this known to us and give us the ability to understand (John 14:26; 15:26; 1 Cor. 2:10–16).

God the Father is not limited in His ability to love us like our frail, finite, earthly fathers. He is our eternal, majestic, mighty yet loving, patient, and long-suffering Creator Father, our source of life. (To read more about our wonderful Father God, read J. I. Packer's *Knowing God*, listed in appendix 3, "Recommended Reading.")

Earthly fathers and our heavenly Father

When you are contemplating the love of God the Father, if you are like me and most every other woman I know, you likely have trouble feeling it consistently. Maybe you experience a profound sense of His love every once in a while, but it's just not a feeling you can count on. While we desire His love because what we know of it is appealing, we don't come to rely on it or trust it. Sadly, we often don't sense the love of God the Father because we get hung up on the words *love* and *father*.

These words mean very different things from one person to the next. That's because each of us gains our understanding of them through our own individual life experiences. When we look at earthly fathers, a wide spectrum of words can be used to describe them—from *kind, thoughtful, loving, patient, compassionate, giving, fun, protective,* and *encouraging* to *distant, intimidating, authoritative, rejecting, unavailable, disapproving, mean,* and *harsh*. The list is as varied as there are different people with fathers! You can see how impossible it is, based on this approach to determining a word's meaning, to expect everyone to have the same feeling or understanding of a father's love.

Think about your relationship with your own father. Be it good, bad, completely nonexistent, or anything in between, we are built in such a way that we transfer that feeling or perception directly onto our heavenly Father. (I am indebted to Dr. Norm Wakefield, a colleague of mine from Phoenix Seminary, for this insight.) If, for example, your earthly father was harsh and judgmental, demanding and guilt producing, you will tend to see God the same way.

As discussed in chapters 2 and 3, it is difficult to change faulty assumptions that have been ingrained in us for so long that they seem like truth. But it *is* possible. When you recognize that your perception of the words *love* and *father* may be inaccurate, it will free you to accept their true definitions as evidenced in God's Word. Any other concept comes from our fallen, corrupt world.

You have an earthly father, and you have a heavenly Father. They are different. Understanding and accepting the differences between the two, and entrusting yourself to your heavenly Father by believing what He says, are the keys to embracing your unique value and true identity.

As adults, it becomes critical that we accept our parents and primary influencers as they were and are, complete with their specific frailties and shortcomings. It takes maturity to seek forgiveness and reconciliation for whatever grievances you may have against them. But as you pursue healing and acceptance of your past, I implore you: don't let any difficulties you may encounter delay you from taking hold of God's love.

Experiencing God's love

It's never too soon to accept and move into the embrace of your loving heavenly Father. You do not have to wait until you feel at peace with your earthly father in order to accept your heavenly Father's love. In fact, as you move into His love, He will equip you with everything you need for life and godliness (2 Pet. 1:3). Healing and wholeness from past hurts is absolutely possible and completely in His will. Our heavenly Father is the Father of reconciliation (2 Cor. 5:18–19).

His love truly is too good to postpone. His love is patient; His love is kind. His love protects and hopes and always perseveres. Read 1 Corinthians 13 for the full definition of true love. This is the love God freely gives you … with absolute abandon. Seek it with boldness and confidence. Ask Him to move you from *head* knowledge of His love to experiential *heart* knowledge. He wants this for you! "You will seek me and find me when you seek me with all your heart" (Jer. 29:13). God will reveal Himself to you who earnestly look for Him. This is His promise.

A. W. Tozer states in his book *The Knowledge of the Holy* that what we think about God is the most important thing about us, and I agree.[5] If your perception of God the Father and the kind of love with which He pursues you is not accurate, your life will reflect this misunderstanding, and you will not live in the fullness of His love as He intended. If you don't think correctly about God, it impacts all areas of your life.

I asked one of my students what evidence she relies upon to tell her she is valuable. She responded, "The Word of God first, then the blessings in my life. I feel valuable when I am in prayer with God, accepting His will. Even when it's hard to hear, it helps me to know He loves me."

Another student, born into a traditional Chinese folk religion family, said that when she was young her parents put her in a Christian school, though they were not themselves Christians.

> All the years from kindergarten through elementary, I had many chances to hear the Gospel. I did not believe in Jesus until I was in the seventh grade. It was during a chapel when the preacher talked about God's love. I was very touched by His love

> because of the lack of my parents' love. So when the preacher made an invitation, I walked up to the stage to confess my faith in Him.
>
> I was an active member in the school fellowship ever since I became a Christian, but there was still no real joy in my life. My behavior was not much different from a non-Christian's. It wasn't until I was in the tenth grade, when my grade point average was one of the lowest in the class, that I fell into great depression. I started to question my beliefs and my behavior. I doubted God's love, and lost my hope in this world. At that critical moment I cried to God, "If you are a true God, help me in my study!" After this prayer I got a 100 percent on my mathematics test. Ever since then, I put my faith totally in God, acknowledging that I am a sinner. He is the most powerful God.

For this woman, her perfect test score was a turning point. It was a simple thing, but profound enough to prove to her the reality of God's presence and love. We don't have to experience a monumental life change to have our life change monumentally. We simply have to be open to noticing tangible evidences of His love.

"You will seek me and find me when you seek me with all your heart."—Jeremiah 29:13

Remember—the Father's love is not a textbook love. It doesn't come in the form of an equation. It's not the forced result of obligation. God is God; He can make any decision He wants. And He has chosen to love you! His love for you is alive, vibrant, and personal. It's fervent, zealous, devoted. It's what motivated Him to create you exquisitely for a calling of eternal significance. "So, chosen by God for this new life of love, dress in the wardrobe God picked out for you" (Col. 3:12, MSG).

Notice that you are *chosen* by God. God has picked you to be His representative, His ambassador, His image bearer. It is a wonderful calling, a tremendous honor. Still don't believe it? Get used to it, because it's true. You get to decide what you wear every day, so keep putting on the wardrobe that He picked out for you. The only thing standing between you and the truth that *you have been created with love by God the Father* is … well, *you*.

Prayer

Father, thank You that Your Word is true. I confess that I have let my own assumptions and experiences keep me from knowing You as my heavenly Father, which has in turn shaped how I see myself. I want to see You for who You truly are, and see myself through Your eyes. I want to grow in a deeper relationship with You as my heavenly Father. Reveal to me more and more each day what it means that I am created with love to bear Your image. Show me what it means to live out my true identity. Amen.

Chapter 5

Created Uniquely Woman

You, woman, are created with love by God the Father. What a profound, liberating truth! You can bank your identity on it. In the last chapter we looked at what it means to be created with love for the purpose of bearing God's image. In this chapter we will look at what it means to be created uniquely woman. Embracing your identity as a woman is important because it is the will and blessing of God.

You are not *accidentally* female (Ps. 139:13); you are not subpar in comparison with men (Gal. 3:28); and your life is not without God's blessing (Gen. 5:2). Both men and women are created in God's image (Gen. 1:27). However, our world perpetuates lies radically opposed to this truth. The world screams from every angle that woman is inferior … that no matter how hard you try, you will forever be "less than."

Male Terminology in Scripture

To get to the point of complete and genuine acceptance of God's truth in a world determined to keep you from it, it is important to address the questions and doubts that threaten to keep you from embracing the goodness of your true identity. A foundational question that haunts many women is their very femininity. They ask, *If I am created in God's image, why is He described throughout Scripture with male terminology? And why are both men and women referred to as "man" in the Bible? Don't these facts make men superior?*

No doubt, *He* and *Him* are the pronouns used throughout the Bible for God. Wayne Grudem says that this "is a practice that originated with God Himself and we should not find it objectionable or insensitive."[1] I agree. Male pronouns have been used to refer to God in the Scriptures since the beginning. When He is described in the written Word, God is assigned anthropomorphic, or humanlike, qualities. We read about His eyes that see and ears that hear, His strong arm and hand, even His back. Scripture uses familiar images because we cannot fully comprehend or relate to a God who is Spirit (John 4:24) and who has no sex and yet created both the male and female sexes.

It is also true that humanity is called "mankind" in the Scriptures. Look at Genesis 1:27: "So God created man in his own image, in the image of God he created him; male and female he created them." Now it says here that man *and* woman are image bearers, but God calls them both "man." This is not meant as something derogatory. This is an inclusive term. When the word *man* is used in Genesis 1:27, it refers to both men and women.

God imbued both sexes with Himself. He made both in His likeness. That includes *both* masculine *and* feminine qualities. Male and female together—the entire spectrum of created people—paint a more complete picture of the reality of God's nature than either one alone. If you view God as strictly male or female, you have a wrong view of God. He is *Spirit.*

God's feminine characteristics are described throughout Scripture, though we tend to miss them. Consider Genesis 3:6–21. After Adam and Eve sin, they discover they are naked and they cover themselves with fig leaves. After God makes it clear how they and the earth will suffer as a consequence of their sin, He then goes to work on their wardrobe. He gets them better outfitted by providing them with animal skins.

Think about that! Isn't that just like a mother to discipline her children and then make sure they know she still loves them? And how better to do so than by giving them a clothing upgrade? Of course there are men who sew and enjoy shopping, but it does tend to be women who take care of children's clothing needs.

Also consider Jesus Christ when He looks out over Jerusalem and laments their rebelliousness. He exclaims, "O Jerusalem, Jerusalem … how often I have longed to gather your children together, as a hen gathers her chicks under her wings" (Matt. 23:37). This is a uniquely female word picture.

God created male and female. Because we are created in His image, we as men and women both represent Him. Men and women have differences and similarities, but together we represent the image of God in the fullness of humanity.

If you view God as strictly
male or female, you have a
wrong view of God.
He is *Spirit.*

Different by Design

It's easy to see and accept differences in our physical bodies, but we often want the differences to stop there. Over the last century, women have been fighting hard to "prove" that they are the same as men. It began in the nonbelieving, secular world where male/female differences are interpreted to mean that one is better than the other. Many Christian women, unfortunately, have also bought into this view. They fail to recognize that while God created both sexes with distinct differences, He warrants them equal value.

These well-meaning but misinformed Christian women join

our liberal culture in advocating sameness and striving to diminish differences. This does both men and women a disservice. We are not the same. In striving to be the same, the cause of women is not advanced; it is pushed back and misses the mark entirely. The entire approach is skewed because it accepts the premise that we are of more value if we become like men.

This concept is not from God. From Genesis to Revelation there is evidence upon evidence of the differences between men and women. (See, for example, Genesis 2:18; 1 Peter 3:7; 1 Thessalonians 2:7.) It is supposed to be this way. Our differences are a gift! Without them, we might as well all be of the same gender. If that were what God had wanted, He would have made it so.

Understanding and embracing our God-given male/female differences increases our personal freedom. When you wholly embrace who God created you to be, you become free to fulfill your calling as a woman bearing His image. By accepting our differences, we also restore power and balance to the community of believers that comprises—you got it!—both men and women. We need to balance the masculine with the feminine. And we can do this whether we are married or single.

Let's examine just a few of the key differences that make us different from our male counterparts. God has built these differences into our very identity as females. As we recognize and embrace them, we are able to use them for God's glory and for the good of those with whom we are in relationship. Living confidently as God's female image bearers, we can understand and appreciate the unique ways God has equipped us and our male counterparts.

Keep in mind as you read about these differences between the sexes that some generalities are used in order to make the points clear. Visualize a bell curve. Most people fall somewhere between the two extremes of male and female; they are a mix of both qualities. Your personality, temperament, environment, cultural and familial influences, gifts, talents, and perspectives all help determine where you fall on the curve of masculine and feminine tendencies. Some women more readily identify with a typically male description (for example, being achievement oriented and less relational) and vice versa. Together, men and women show a more complete picture of what God is like than just men or just women do. We show elements of Him that the other gender does not manifest as clearly.

Helper, Sustainer, Warrior

Where does God first acknowledge that something is "not good" in the world that He created? You might think it was when sin entered the picture, but it was before that. It's in Genesis 2:18: "The LORD God said, 'It is not good for the man to be alone. I will make a helper suitable for him.'"

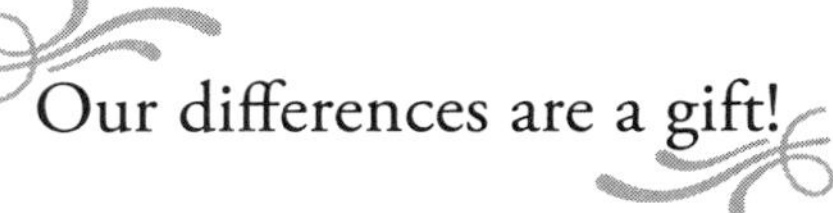

Adam was in relationship with God, but he had no one like himself, no counterpart he could relate to. Adam was alone from God's perspective, even though God was there. God saw the problem and could have created another man for Adam, a buddy for him to pal around with. But instead, He formed a whole new gender, one with different qualities that complement man's, so that together they make humanity complete.

The word *helper* used in the NIV translation above comes from the original Hebrew word *ezer*. (Genesis was originally written in Hebrew.) *Ezer* can be translated to mean *helper, companion, help-*

meet, and even *lifesaver*. As a Hebrew military term the word *ezer* also means "strong helper" or "warrior."

> The word ezer appears about twenty-two times in the Old Testament, and eighteen of those times it is used of God. Always referring to 'a significant helper like God, a king, a prince, or a great warrior, the word ezer underscores how critical the helper is. It is someone who is of critical importance, who normally will deliver another from an immense problem, and who is a loyal companion. Being a magnificent term, it is not the Hebrew word for a slave, a hireling, an assistant, or a vice-president. We would not say to God, 'God, you are my assistant.' But instead, God is our ezer, our helper. God said, 'I will make him a *helper* suitable for him [or who is his complement].' Because the helper was able to harmoniously match him, it really meant she was a magnificent helper who was his equal.[2]

Kenegdo is the Hebrew word used in Genesis 2:18, translated above as "suitable." It encompasses the descriptors *counterpart, alongside, corresponding to, complement,* etc. When these two Hebrew words *ezer* and *kenegdo* are used together, Hebrew scholar Robert Alter suggests the phrase "ezer kenegdo" means "sustainer beside him."[3] And so by reading Genesis 2, we come to understand why the first woman was created. Woman was created to be an awesome helper, an equal, someone who sustains man (think about where children come from) and complements him, who is a companion, someone beside man helping him. Wow! What a great job!

Author and Christian men's speaker John Eldredge says, "You need an ezer in your life if your life is in constant danger."[4] And as believers our lives are in constant spiritual danger. We live in enemy territory. Carolyn Custis James emphasizes the "warrior" translation of *ezer* and sees our role as women as that of Christian soldiers made to battle alongside man, our partner, and/or alongside men in the Body of Christ.[5]

As women we are life givers, life sustainers, helpers, and warriors fighting for the Kingdom of God. We are complementary to men. There is a mutual dependence between man and woman whether you are married or not. We need each other. This is the reality built into you by our heavenly, relational Father. When men and women are teamed, be it in the context of marriage or as neighbors, friends, coworkers, or fellow servants of God, we fulfill His intention for creation.

Relationally Oriented

From the first woman of all time to today's twenty-first century woman, women tend to define themselves in context of relationships. Men, on the other hand, most often define themselves in terms of individual achievement. This gives biblical credence to the woman being created to come alongside man. She is by nature relationally oriented. Of course both are created for relationship, but woman is uniquely designed to nurture and sustain, while man is uniquely designed to pursue and achieve. The two fit together perfectly. This is God's design.

Carol Gilligan, author of *In a Different Voice*, tells the result of her study of women:

> In response to the request to describe themselves, all of the women describe a relationship, depicting their identity in the connection of future mother, present wife, adopted child, or past lover. Similarly, the standard of moral judgment that informs their assessment of self is a standard of relationship, an ethic of nurturance, responsibility and care. Measuring their strength in the acidity of attachment ("giving to," "helping out," "being kind," "not hurting"), these highly successful and achieving women do not mention their academic and professional distinction in the context of describing themselves. If anything, they regard their professional activities as jeopardizing their own sense of themselves, and the conflict they encounter between achievement and care leaves them either divided in judgment or feeling betrayed. Thus in all of the women's descriptions, identity is defined in a context of relationship and judged by a standard of responsibility and care.[6]

How do we see this played out? You can probably think of numerous examples in your own life from the working world, at home, and in school. It all starts when we are young. Girls are invested in preserving harmonious relationships, and boys are invested in accomplishing goals.

Together, men and women show a more complete picture of what God is like than just men or just women do.

Dr. Louann Brizendine, a neuropsychiatrist at the University of California San Francisco, studies women and the differences in their brain function from men. In her book, *The Female Brain,* she writes about a woman who gave her three-year-old daughter unisex toys because she didn't want to bend her daughter in one direction or another. This woman tried giving her daughter a little red toy fire truck instead of a doll. One afternoon the mother found the girl cuddling the truck in a baby blanket, rocking it back and forth saying, "Don't worry, little trucky, everything will be all right."[7] It is a feminine quality to nurture.

Brizendine writes, "[The t]ypical non-testosteronized, estrogen-ruled girls are very invested in preserving harmonious relationships. From their earliest days, they live most comfortably and happily in the realm of peaceful interpersonal connections. They prefer to avoid conflict because discord puts them at odds with their urge to stay connected, to gain approval and nurture."[8] (See 1 Samuel 25 for an example of a woman who stepped in to resolve a conflict between two men.)

Today's scientific studies and findings are proving what God has made clear from the very beginning. In Genesis we see that God designed us for relationship, and He created male and female different in significant ways. It's no accident that you get flustered or disturbed when there is discord or conflict. You have been designed to seek social harmony!

In my studies and as a people helper, I have observed what marriage experts tell us regarding the marriage life cycle. Early on, the woman is intensely interested in developing intimacy with her husband. She wants to foster that relationship by spending a lot of time with him. The man, on the other hand, wants to discover himself and achieve, and does so by pursuing his personal goals. Achievement is his primary focus at this point, not developing that close personal relationship young wives desire. Men usually awaken to the desire for emotional intimacy with their partner later in life.

As married couples progress in years, a shift occurs. The man turns home, desiring to focus on his relationship with his wife, but by that point the wife is often saying, "I've got stuff to do. I was ready fifteen years ago, and you were busy. Now I'm busy."

It's generally acknowledged that the two most common points at which a couple will divorce is within the first three years of marriage or after the kids have left home. It's unfortunate because the simple remedy—not only for marriages but in male/female relationships of every kind—is a mutual understanding of this fundamental difference between male and female. We are simply different.

Woman is uniquely designed to nurture and sustain, while man is uniquely designed to pursue and achieve.

Our Brains Are Not the Same

Scientific studies using modern technology bear physical proof of biblical reality in explaining our different behavior. PET and MRI scans enable scientists to observe real, live human brains in real time. "Scientists have documented an astonishing array of structural, chemical, genetic, hormonal and functional brain differences between men and women."[9] And what do the findings show but that men and women are born with hardwired, innate differences ... just as God designed.

The fascinating differences in our brains actually shed much light on things that have been frustrating women about men, and vice versa, throughout the ages. Consider the evidence that follows.

"By all standards, men are on average twenty times more aggressive than women, something that a quick look around the prison system will confirm."[10] Certainly stress and conflict are handled differently by male and female brains, and I doubt you needed me to tell you that. We use "different brain areas and circuits to solve problems, process language, and experience and store the same strong emotion."[11]

"In the brain centers for language and hearing ... women have 11 percent more neurons than men. The principal hub of both emotion and memory formation—the hippocampus—is also larger in the female brain, as is the brain circuitry for language and observing emotions in others. This means that women are on average better at expressing emotions and remembering details about emotional events."[12]

The emotion may be the same—anger, hope, frustration, disappointment, or any one of hundreds of emotions—but the way it is processed and stored means a very different response on the part of the man or woman experiencing it. And because our memory centers are different, you may remember all the details of your first date with your husband, while he scarcely remembers that it happened. If you want to fault him, fault his brain!

Men also "have two and a half times the brain space devoted to sexual drive," so sexual thoughts will cross a man's mind many times a day but through a woman's usually only once a day.[13] If you want to fault him for this, again—fault his brain. It's a real, live, human organ—not a personality flaw—and it's different than yours.

Finally, lest you think we are completely foreign creatures, men and women are actually genetically much alike. "Human beings have twenty-three pairs of chromosomes, totaling forty-six. Out of the twenty-three, one pair consists of the sex chromosomes, the only chromosomes that differ between man and woman. A man has an X chromosome and Y chromosome, whereas a woman has two X chromosomes."[14] When a child is conceived, since a woman contributes only the X chromosome, the man's sperm, a combination of the X and Y chromosomes, determines the child's gender. (This is interesting in light of the immense pressure put on women throughout history in various cultures to birth boys.)

We Communicate Differently

You don't need to be told that men and women communicate differently. You have experienced this reality just by being alive and interacting with the other half of the human population. These communication differences have caused havoc and wreaked relational woes for ages. The problem is not that one party is right and the other is wrong, but that both parties fail to acknowledge, accept, and adjust accordingly to these fundamental differences.

In recent years, books and classes on communication between the sexes have dramatically increased in number, shedding light and granting both parties valuable insights. Relationships are healing and strengthening as a result.

The first of our many different communication methods is that we women typically see conversation as a relationship-building event. For us, it's a process to be enjoyed. Men typically communicate in order to accomplish a goal. For them, it's a task to be done. They will talk to solve a problem, win a game, or get from point A to point B. We will talk, well, just to talk! We talk in order to build the relationship, not to achieve a goal.

A man's brain is a real, live, human organ—not a personality flaw—and it's different than yours.

Don't be fooled into thinking this means men don't have or want relationships and conversation. They do. But the way they go about it is different. Men build relationships by working together on a task or doing something with a specific goal in mind, such as hiking a mountain, fixing a car, or watching a basketball game. Men generally don't call each other just to chat or to ask, "Can we hang out on Saturday morning for an hour or two?" Women are more inclined to call "just to catch up," or say, "Hey, I haven't seen you for a while. Come on over and we'll have coffee together." Coffee isn't the point, of course; the relationship-building conversation is.

Perhaps you've heard the expression that women tend to be face-to-face, while men are shoulder-to-shoulder. This offers an image of two women facing each other for the purpose of communicating, and a picture of men standing side-by-side as they work on accomplishing something together. Men generally feel freer to communicate and share their lives when a task is being accomplished. (Again, remember the bell curve I mentioned.)

Another female tendency in communication is our use of facial expression. This starts when we are young. Science again is proving God's design. Anita Sethi, PhD, a research scientist at the Child and Family Policy Center at New York University, says, "Girls are more likely to establish and maintain eye contact, and are attracted to individual faces—especially women's. They're also more skilled at reading emotional expressions. Boys take longer to notice the difference, according to a meta-analysis of twenty-six studies on kids' capacity to recognize facial expressions."[15]

Have you ever wondered why when you look sad, the men in your life don't seem to notice? I used to try to communicate when I was feeling down by giving my husband a really sorry look. He would never pick up on it. The only thing he might have noticed was that something was wrong with my face. I have since learned to come out and specifically say, "Hey, I'm sad right now."

Women use their faces to give nonverbal feedback to a speaker. When I'm teaching a class of women, my students look me in the eye, nod their heads, and smile. They are affirming that they're following what I'm saying. My experience is much different when I teach classes of men. They do not give nearly as many nonverbal cues. Men tend to be straight-faced, not wanting to reveal what they are thinking through facial expressions.

I've been in meetings where a man presents his opinion on an issue and a woman gives him the typical female affirmative responses. When it comes time to vote and she votes against his idea, the man feels deceived. He thought she was agreeing with him, while she thought she was giving him due respect as a speaker. He thought she was "tricking" him, while she thought she was affirming his contribution. This goes back to a woman's relational orientation and a man's task orientation.

Another communication difference is a woman's propensity to use questions and taglines. Linguist Robin Lakoff first pointed this out, and Jacqueline Sachs, observing the language of children as young as two to five, found that girls used more than twice as many tag questions as boys.[16] Women will be indirect, phrasing statements and ideas as questions. For example, when we know we need bread, we say, "What do you think if we swing by the store on the way home?" Or, "If you have time, would you mind picking up some bread at the store?" Even opinions are expressed with an opening tagline like "I think" and followed by a question such as "okay?" or "you know?"

Our differences are a fact not to be fought, but embraced.

Men hear this as uncertainty. But women do it to keep the playing field "flat," in order to foster equality and openness—which of course points back to our goal of nurturing the relationship.

Our Social Structure Is "Flat" and His Is Not

A brother and sister typically grow up in different worlds, even when they are raised in the same household. His is the male culture, hers is the female culture. Boys learn and grow playing competitively. Girls grow up learning to share. Boys learn to thrive in a hierarchical form of social organization. Girls flourish in a flat structure, or on a level playing field, so to speak.

What do I mean by this? Consider the athletic environment. In football boys can knock each other down one minute and walk off the field arm in arm to get pizza together the next. On the field it's about winning. The coach gives the orders; the players carry them out. The team is built on a command-and-control structure. Everyone learns to play their position and do what the coach tells them to do. For men, being a team player means playing your position well and executing the orders you're given.

I'm not saying girls don't play sports; I'm using the analogy to show the hierarchical, top-down culture that is the norm for boys. As they become men, they continue to see the world through this hierarchical filter. Girls, even if athletic and involved in sports, grow up in a relationally "flat" culture. They often play games, "house," or other activities where everyone has an equal say. A girl's idea of teamwork is where everyone gives input and asks questions before a decision is made. Maintaining relationships, facilitating camaraderie, and reaching a consensus remain important as girls grow up and become women.[17]

Can you see how easily the two sexes, while they may be physically in the same environment, will see the world differently, as though from foreign cultures? For example, consider a time when you asked questions of a man (remember our tendency to phrase ideas and thoughts in question form) and he reacted defensively, as though he was being challenged. It's not that he wants to be rude; it's that he experiences your questions as a challenge to his authority. He feels disrespected. While you aren't trying to challenge him, and may actually be trying to enhance the relationship, he takes offense.

Consider what these different cultures mean for male/female relationships in various environments such as the workplace, committee meetings, home, church, and other social activities. The man usually interacts with others from a top-down mentality, and the woman approaches everyone as equal. Both perspectives have benefits and drawbacks, depending on the context. In the home, for example, a husband and wife must relate to one another differently than a coach and athlete would on the field.

Communication problems arise when women function in a flat or equal relational environment, men function in a hierarchical structure … and neither recognizes it. Good communication between men and women hinges on the understanding that we live in different social structures, and that we are designed to have these differences.

This was God's plan from the beginning (Gen. 1:27). Our differences are a fact not to be fought, but embraced. We can remain true to our identity while bridging the communication gap with men, joyfully embracing who we are and celebrating our differences.

These are only a few of the awesome and creative, pointed and unique ways that you, being made female, reflect God's image. And you were created this way with love by your Father! I hope you discover more and more of the characteristics that define you as God's female image bearer. Recognizing these distinctions will free you to become wholly who God made you to be, something we will examine more closely in the last part of this book.

Prayer

Father, "I praise you because I am fearfully and wonderfully made; Your works are wonderful, I know that full well" (Ps. 139:14). Thank You for making me equal to and distinct from my male counterparts. I ask You to reveal more ways You have made me uniquely female, that I might come to know You and Your purposes for me. Help me to embrace them with grace and gratitude. Amen.

Chapter 6

Elevated by the Son

In the movie *Beaches,* Bette Midler delivers one of my all-time favorite lines: "But enough about me, let's talk about you … what do you think of me?" As is so often the case, the humor in the comment is rooted in a fundamental truth about human nature—we all want to feel significant. The more humble among us may not come out and say it in so many words, but this is in fact a universal need among human beings. A part of being alive is the desire to find meaning and feel worthwhile, needed, important … *significant.*

This need is depicted in the "esteem" level of Abraham Maslow's hierarchy of human needs pyramid. Maslow, an American psychologist, shed scientific light on our God-given design. He opened the eyes of the secular world to that which God had already made clear in His Word: that we humans are created with the desire to have a place and purpose in this world. We want to know our significance beyond the shadow of a doubt, and to take confidence in it.

This need cannot be met in a vacuum, however. God the Father in His sovereign, all-knowing, infinite wisdom knows the frailty of humanity. He knows that creating us in His image may not be all that we need to understand our value in Him. He knows we are prone to search high and low, near and far to fill this need. And He knows our desire is insatiable. But He also knows our need to be valued is perfectly met in Him alone.

> We humans are created with the desire to have a place and purpose in this world.

And so He chose His Son, a man who never did anything without being in harmony with the Father, to meet this need within us. Through the Person of Jesus Christ, God elevates women and makes tangible the truth that we are His image bearers of invaluable worth. Through Jesus Christ we find both our earthly and our eternal significance.

Who Is Jesus Christ?

Jesus is the second Person of the Trinity. He is God the Father's perfect Son. He was sent by the Father, and He is in perfect unity with the Father (John 17). He revealed Himself in the flesh, made His dwelling among us, and accomplished victory over sin and death. He became the only sacrifice acceptable to God for our sin (1 John 2:1–2; John 14:6).

But two thousand years ago in a humble barn in Bethlehem is not when Christ came into existence. Christ was with God at the very beginning of time (John 1). That means that in the creation account in Genesis we have been studying, it wasn't just God as Father creating the first man and woman, it was God as Father, Son, and Holy Spirit.

The implications of this simple fact are profound. It means that when Christ walked this earth, He was the Creator stepping into His creation. As the One who created us, He completely understood us. We often think of God as Creator and Jesus as man. We disconnect the two who were and are one and the same.

Entering into His own creation, Jesus was well aware of the restrictive, deprecating culture in which women were living at the time of His birth (review chapter 3). And He knew very well the fallen state of mankind, including man's failure to place due value and significance upon women. He knew the lack of self-worth women harbor deep within their being as a result.

As He walked the earth teaching and ministering, Jesus—in perfect harmony with God the Father—consistently debunked the world's faulty view of women. The Bible does not record Him speaking directly on the plight of women, but it does record many of His interactions with them. You have heard it said that actions speak louder than words, and indeed His did. Jesus elevated women, communicating their value as female image bearers. He not only honored women, He assigned them a significant role in His Kingdom work. His behavior toward women was completely unexpected and countercultural.

Reading the New Testament today, it is easy to miss how radically inappropriate, according to the customs and attitudes of the time, was Christ's treatment of women. He reestablished their incomparable worth and value. No man had yet gone to the extremes that Christ did to elevate women. In this chapter we will examine His interactions with and teachings about women that truly define Jesus Christ as a "radical rabbi." You will see how, through His life, the burden that women have been bearing through the centuries since Eve has been decisively and completely broken—once and for all.

This chapter is not merely a history lesson. Jesus Christ is alive today! He lives and is interceding on your behalf right now (Rom. 8:34). There are no chains left for any woman to bear. All of this means that today *you are free.*

Jesus Defies Culture: The Woman at the Well

Jesus assigned women new freedom, status, and roles. He began reforming the Jewish patriarchal system as it had been established in the Old Testament. When you read John 4:1–30, you see an account of Jesus' interaction with a Samaritan woman at a water well, and it reveals just how radically His actions flew in the face of society. He rejected several rabbinical teachings in this passage, and His behavior made no sense to those around him.

Starting with verse 3 we read, "When the Lord learned of this, he left Judea and went back once more to Galilee." Galilee is north of Judea with Samaria in between. The Jews wouldn't step foot in Samaria if they could possibly help it. There was a long-standing hatred between Jews and Samaritans. The Samaritans were a mixed-race people, half Assyrian and half Jewish, and their religion was a mixture of Judaism and other beliefs. Any mixing of the Jewish race or their religion was detested by the Jews. This hatred was so common, a well-known rabbinical ordinance stated, "Let no Israelite eat one mouthful of anything that is a Samaritan's, for if he eats but a mouthful, he is as if he ate swine's flesh."[1] Swine was an unclean food, forbidden for Jews to eat. The Jews considered the Samaritans to be unclean, just like pork.

To avoid going through Samaria, Jews would walk an extra seventeen miles to cross the Jordan and go around—basically doubling the length of the journey. Still today, two thousand years later, there are Jews who refuse to go through certain portions of the land. But verse 4 tells us that Jesus *"had* to go through Samaria" (emphasis mine). When any good Jew would not step foot in Samaria but instead went a considerable extra distance to avoid doing so, this statement should prompt us to ask *why?* Apparently, Jesus had a God-ordained appointment with a woman who needed to know Him.

When Christ walked this earth,
He was the Creator stepping
into His creation.

Now consider the Samaritan woman. Today she would be called a loser. She was seen as such by her community because she had been married five times and was considered immoral. To the Jews she was inferior because she was of mixed race, the wrong religion, a female, and to top it off, she was living an immoral life. She was "defective goods." While she had been married many times, we do not know whether the immorality was her fault. Divorce law weighed heavily in favor of men, and some of her husbands may have just put her out of the house. Or maybe they were killed in battles. We do not know.

Regardless, the culture defined her as an outcast to be ignored and shunned. Consider her self-image. Who did she think she was? She must have felt pretty low. On a scale ranging from one to ten, she possibly felt a zero. She was used, abused, and alienated—just as so many women have been through the ages and still are around the world today. Perhaps you identify closely with this woman.

The woman came to the well alone in the middle of the day, which was an unusual time to collect water. The well was a gathering place, a social hub. The women of the village would gather there in the mornings to retrieve their water for the day. But this Samaritan likely felt rejected by her peers and was trying to make do with life on the bottom rung of the social ladder by becoming invisible. So she went to the well when she was sure no one else would be there.

Cultural & Traditional Dictated Behavior	The Radical Rabbi's Behavior
A rabbi could not speak to a woman in public.	Christ speaks to a Samaritan woman. Christ rejected Jewish teaching forbidding talking to women.
Jewish leaders considered women incapable of understanding religious teaching.	Christ thought she was capable of learning.
Jewish leaders considered a woman unworthy of religious teaching.	Christ thought she was worthy and wanted to include her in the plan of salvation.
Women were not considered reliable witnesses in Israel.	Christ knew she would be a witness for Him.
Rabbinic law stated that Samaritan women were considered unclean.	Christ defied this tradition. He rejected Jewish teaching regarding uncleanness.
Religious segregation was normal for both women and Samaritans.	Christ defied this tradition.
A man would never drink from a woman's cup.	Christ asked to drink from her cup.
A rabbi would not associate with sinners.	Christ associated with her.

And then culture came head-to-head with Christ's behavior. Consider the ways this encounter was so radical, and how many man-made rules He broke. Most striking, rabbinical law stated that Samaritan women were considered unclean. Jesus rejected this Jewish teaching by reaching out to a mixed-race female (that's two strikes against her), *and* one whose morality was in question. It would never cross the mind of any "good Jew" to treat this person as a fellow human being.

Secondly, a godly Jewish man, let alone a rabbi (teacher), was not to speak to a woman in public. Men simply did not speak to women in public. In fact, a husband would not even address his wife if he saw her on the street! Yet Jesus, a revered rabbi, willingly initiates conversation with this down-and-out, mixed-race female at one of the village's social hot spots.

Thirdly, religious segregation was standard for both women and Samaritans. Not only would a Jewish man never drink from a woman's cup, a rabbi would never even associate with a "sinner." Think now about how Jesus opened his conversation with the Samaritan woman by asking to have a drink from her cup! This surely alarmed her. He asked to drink from the cup of a woman viewed by the culture to be in a constant state of uncleanness. That's radical! His request would have been like a white man drinking from a fountain marked "colored only" in Alabama in the 1950s. But here, Jesus Christ Himself not only asks for a drink, He engages in a lengthy conversation with a woman "sinner" ... in public.

We also know that Jewish leaders of the day considered a woman incapable of a religious education. Jesus engaged her on a deep spiritual level of conversation almost immediately, challenging her understanding of religious teachings. She tried to keep the conversation at the surface, asking about the proper place for worship. Jesus let her ask, but then gently guided her back to a level where He could engage her heart. He taught her that what was really important was not where you worship, but whether you worship in spirit and in truth. That was pretty deep for a conversation at a well.

Not only did Jewish leaders consider a woman incapable of a

religious education, they saw her as *unworthy*. Jesus deemed her capable *and* worthy of learning … worthy enough to offer her salvation. He tells her that if she knew the gift of God and who it was asking her for a drink, she would have asked Him and He would have given her living water. Jesus invited her into God's eternal plan.

Finally, women were not considered reliable witnesses in Israel. If Jesus had wanted to spread His Good News through a "respectable" method, He would have had such an encounter with a man. Instead, He chose a Samaritan woman so changed by their interaction that the first thing she does is witness to her community. She runs and shouts throughout the village, "Come, see a man who told me everything I ever did. Could this be the Christ?" (verse 29). The Samaritan woman goes from avoiding people in the morning to seeking them out in the afternoon! What happened to her? Do you think her view of herself was changed? What happened to the shame she surely must have felt earlier that same day?

Jesus consistently debunked the world's faulty view of women.

On so many levels Jesus defied tradition and culture in this encounter. Before they met, this woman felt alienated, used, and abused. But in one brief conversation she is given a profound message about her true value—one she had likely never heard in all her years. Through their encounter she became both a member and a messenger of God's Kingdom. Jesus changed her life! She was liberated, His redeemed image bearer. She received and responded to His unconditional acceptance of her. This is how Jesus Christ wants to change you today.

Think about Fadua, the Moroccan I mentioned in chapter 3. She said that she did not think anything about Christ because thinking and believing were things for men, not women. Well, that was not the end of her story. When she heard that she is significant to Christ, that she is valuable to God, her entire face changed. She lit up. She smiled with the wonder that she could possibly be important to someone. This is the reality of the significance Christ lives to bring women today.

Jesus Forgives Women: The Woman Caught in Adultery

Through His encounter with the Samaritan woman, Christ communicated an open invitation to experience Him and become involved in God's Kingdom work. He excludes no one; *all* women fit the bill. As He walked this earth He touched people in every stratum of society. He elevated the marginalized and disenfranchised.

Consider how He challenges the scribes and Pharisees, the teachers of the religious law, in John 8:1–11. They bring before Him a woman "caught in the act of adultery" (verse 4). Right there, you can't help but wonder, *Who was watching, anyway? Why didn't they bring the man, too?* The passage doesn't answer those questions, but it clearly states the Pharisees' motive for bringing her to Christ is "as a trap, in order to have a basis for accusing him" (verse 6).

We see how beautifully Jesus handles the situation when He kneels down to draw in the dirt. This seems to be a bizarre response. But it serves Christ's purpose to quickly and quietly avert everyone's attention from the woman and onto Himself. You can imagine if she has literally just been "caught in the act," she is likely naked, or close to it. Perhaps wrapped in a piece of fabric, she is probably shivering, humiliated, and ashamed. We don't know how many pair of eyes from the growing crowd bore into her.

But as Christ writes on the ground, He takes the burden of those accusatory stares off her. His response is subtle but convicting: "If any one of you is without sin, let him be the first to throw a stone at her" (verse 7). Their own sin is the last thing on the minds of these men at that moment. But when Christ puts it so succinctly, each man realizes he would be the hypocrite if he threw a stone. So they leave, one by one. Finally, when no one is left, Jesus tells her that He will not condemn her, and she should leave her life of sin. How do you think this affects her view of herself?

In facing off with the Pharisees (not to mention winning), Jesus defends this woman who has been judged and shunned by society. He protects, lifts up, forgives, and blesses her. It is a powerful picture of how He responds to us when we come before Him feeling like we deserve nothing but the worst.

Jesus Elevates Women: Accounts from the Gospel of Luke

The book of Luke gives many examples of how Jesus elevates women from their low standing in society, and their even lower view of themselves. Throughout the book of Luke, the writer makes a strong case for women. He depicts men and women as brothers and sisters standing side by side, equal before God as redeemed disciples. "He stresses again and again that women are among the oppressed that Jesus came to liberate."[2]

Luke 4:16–21 records Jesus standing in the synagogue to read from the scroll of Isaiah. The section He reads (Isa. 61:1–2) is brief: "The Spirit of the Lord is on me, because he has anointed me to preach good news to the poor. He has sent me to proclaim freedom for the prisoners and recovery of sight for the blind, to release the oppressed, to proclaim the year of the Lord's favor" (Luke 4:18–19). He then declares the Scriptures fulfilled that day in their hearing (verse 21), which means that He asserted Himself as the very Messiah prophesied to come.

Think about the poor people for whom Jesus was anointed to share the Good News. Who are among them? Women. What about the captives Jesus came to free? Women are included. And the physically handicapped whom Jesus came to heal? Women. The oppressed He came to liberate? Women. He proves Himself time and time again in both word and deed. The Gospels record only some of these accounts, as He actually did much more than what's recorded in the Bible (John 21:25). For the purposes of this book, we are examining a few of these.

You don't have to be poor to be moved by the way Christ honors a poor widow in Luke 21:1–4. Not only does He avoid praising the offerings of the rich, He holds up the widow and recognizes her as a role model. "She out of her poverty put in all she had to live on" (verse 4). Valuing her sacrificial giving, He establishes her example as the standard to which the wealthy and affluent should aspire! Talk about turning the world's logic upside down.

Jesus changed her life!

It was revolutionary to see women honored as messengers of God and standing right alongside men in their new faith. "It is Elizabeth and Mary, not Zechariah and Joseph, who are first to receive the message of Christ's coming, who are praised and blessed by God's angels, and who are first to sing and prophesy about the Christ child. Luke presents these women not only as witnesses to the events surrounding the births of John and Jesus, but also as active participants in God's Messianic purposes."[3] This was a radical new worldview back then, a radical new way of relating to women.

Jesus also elevates women in the parables He tells. In Luke 18:1–8, He uses another widow, again someone low on the social totem pole, to serve as a role model of persistence. "To show them that they should always pray and not give up" (verse 1), Jesus chooses to describe a woman.

The NIV titles Luke 7:36–50, "Jesus Anointed by a Sinful Woman." Here we find Him at a Pharisee's house for dinner when "a woman who had lived a sinful life" comes in and kneels down, weeping at His feet. You can imagine the sound of her sobs, the odors of food and perfume in the room, and the striking sight of her wetting Christ's feet with her tears and anointing them with perfume. The whole scene is pretty dramatic. It's easy to see how the Pharisee would be appalled. Culture teaches us social norms, and this would be unacceptable. But it wasn't to Christ.

He defends this woman, a sinner. Not in a few words, but many. Three times He acknowledges her to His dinner host, saying, "*You* did not give me any water for my feet, but *she* wet my feet with her tears and wiped them with her hair. *You* did not give me a kiss, but *this woman*, from the time I entered, has not stopped kissing my feet. *You* did not put oil on my head, but *she* has poured perfume on my feet (Luke 7:44–46, emphasis mine).

To really drive home His message, He says, "Therefore, I tell you, her many sins have been forgiven—for she loved much. But he who has been forgiven little loves little" (Luke 7:47). The woman, having been branded immoral and unworthy, is forgiven and redeemed by Jesus Christ. He loves and accepts every sincere, repentant heart.

In Christ's day, although women could attend synagogue and even be well educated if married to a rabbi, they were not generally seen as educable, let alone worthy of an education. But Jesus never subscribed to that view. Luke 10:38–42 records a story that is well known among busy, type-A women today. In this passage Martha opens her home to Jesus and gets right to work, striving to be the perfect hostess. Her sister, on the other hand, sits down at Christ's feet to listen to everything He has to say. This was the customary position for a rabbi's student, and Jesus endorses Mary's chosen place before Him. "Jesus makes clear that for women as well as men, one's primary task is to be a proper disciple."[4]

His response reveals His relational nature; He values a woman's heart more than her outward efforts to please. He affirms a woman's desire to learn, showing He is delighted to teach them and have them become disciples. "Martha's service is not denigrated but it does not come first. Luke portrays Mary as a disciple sitting and learning at the feet of her Master, and as such she serves as a model for his audience."[5]

Christ's ways caused the world around him to do a double take. His radical, countercultural behavior declared, "Women are significant!" and His actions elevated the first-century woman's status in Palestine. This is what He did back then and there, and it is what He continues to do here and now—everywhere around the world today.

Jesus Heals Women: The Woman Healed of Bleeding

Jesus performed many miraculous physical healings. Females young and old were among those He cured and restored to life. In so doing, He afforded women new dignity and respect. These healings ranged from curing minor ailments like the fever Jesus rebuked in Simon's mother-in-law (Luke 4:38–39) to astounding miracles such as healing a crippled woman on the Sabbath (Luke 13:10–17), casting out demons (Luke 8:2), and resurrecting a dead little girl (Mark 5:35–43). In all these cases, Jesus brought wholeness and life to women. Healing and life, value and significance, are what He offers *all* of humanity … including *you*.

Of His many healings, consider Mark 5:21–34, where we are introduced to a hemorrhaging woman. She had not stopped bleeding for *twelve years* though she'd tried everything to find a cure. Nothing helped. She was getting worse. According to Jewish custom and ceremonial law, her bleeding meant she was in a constant state of uncleanness (Lev. 15:19–20).

He loves and accepts every
sincere, repentant heart.

"[A] priest had to be holy and ritually clean at all times in order to offer the sacrifice,"[6] so women were excluded from the temple whenever they had their period. This also meant they were excluded from participating in feasts and festivals because they couldn't be depended upon to be "clean."[7] Uncleanness was associated with sin, and anyone who touched a menstruating woman was also considered unclean. Consequently, the woman in this passage was a social outcast—society's exile. Of all women, she certainly knew great suffering physically, socially, spiritually, and economically.

Put yourself in her place. How humiliating it would be to live as she did, lonely and isolated. Imagine not having human touch for twelve years! Imagine everyone viewing you as dirty. The alienation must have been devastating. After trying doctor after doctor, she was desperate. She had nothing to lose by reaching out for Jesus. The crowd was both an obstacle and a blessing—it would be difficult to reach Him, but if she did she could probably touch Him without Him even noticing.

She made it to Him, and as her fingers grazed the hem of His cloak, she immediately experienced His healing power. You know how good it feels to be well after an illness gets you down for a couple of weeks … imagine twelve years. The relief must have been indescribable.

But suddenly Jesus stopped walking and asked, "Who touched my clothes?" (verse 30). You would think that He would have graciously kept walking and let her stay anonymous. Why draw attention to an outcast? The woman, however, knew He was referring to her and not any of the others pressing against Him because her bleeding had stopped. She balked.

He said again, "Who touched me?" He wasn't going to let this pass. So she dropped to her knees and confessed that she was the one He had healed, something no one else had been able to do in all her years of suffering.

Jesus seized the moment to show the crowd just how precious this woman, this down-and-outer, truly was. You can sense the warmth that must have been in His eyes and see the smile on His face as He kindly and lovingly said, "Daughter, your faith has healed you. Go in peace and be freed from your suffering" (verse 34).

Jesus did not consider it a defilement to be touched by this woman in need, even though culture and tradition declared her untouchable. He dealt another blow to discriminatory traditions! He affirmed her faith and elevated her as a role model. She went from being on the lowest societal rung to being completely healed, lifted up, and honored by the Lord. Not only was she released from her status as an outcast, she was immortalized for her faith.

Jesus Empowers Women

By the norms of the day, Christ's actions throughout Scripture were scandalous! But He went about uninhibited. He healed and helped, forgave and lifted up, loved and blessed women. He even empowered them for a life of ministry. While society placed women among the lowest of the low and Jewish leaders made women out to be incapable and unworthy of a religious education, Jesus intentionally included women in His Kingdom work. Reaching out to society's outcasts made a most profound statement: Jesus freely brings personal significance to each of us and offers eternal life for *all*.

As He traveled from place to place sharing the Good News, guess who joined Him and His twelve disciples? Yes, women (Luke 8:1–3). He valued their company and partnership in ministry. This was radical! Remember, women were not used to having a public presence. Their lives were lived primarily at home. Now Christ was including them in ministry partnership alongside men. He assigned both genders responsibility and influence as His partners in sharing the Good News.

He also empowered women as His witnesses. Just as the Samaritan woman ran to town shouting and testifying about Him (John 4:28–29), so too did the women tell others when they discovered He had risen from the dead. Women were the first to discover His empty tomb (Luke 24:1–12), and the resurrected Christ "appeared first to Mary Magdalene" (Mark 16:9). He wanted women to spread the greatest news in the history of time! It goes to show what a radical concept this was when we see that none of the men believed what they said (Mark 16:11; Luke 24:11). Men were accustomed to dismissing a woman's testimony. But if Christ had agreed, He never would have entrusted women with this task.

Jesus intentionally included women in His Kingdom work.

Time and time again, as Jesus walked the earth teaching and loving, interacting with and ministering to people, He never failed to communicate significance to women. His intentions and character are consistent. While people look at the exterior, He looks at the heart. While the world may shame you for being a woman, He elevates you. While people love conditionally, He loves unconditionally. When men, women, and the whole of society degrade you, He reminds you of your priceless value.

Jesus treated women with dignity, and not because He had to. If He had wanted to be a people pleaser, He would have abided by the customs and cultures of the day that shunned women. But He did exactly the opposite. He believed women are valuable and significant. He envisioned a positive future for women, and He elevated them for a life of meaning and contribution. Through their encounters with Christ, women found significance, equality of personhood, and salvation.

It's no wonder there are a lot of women in the church today. In America, polls and surveys show more women attend and are involved in church than men. That's likely because women are more prone to feel marginalized than men. We respond on a personal level to Christ in His love for us. We are naturally drawn to His unconditional, complete, and positive acceptance. Men may not feel the same intensity of need because they live in a world that favors them. Women, living in a man's world, are more prone to feelings of alienation. When Someone dispels that feeling and gives our lives meaning and significance, we are profoundly affected and attracted to Him.

> Perhaps it is no wonder that women were first at the cradle and last at the cross. They had never known a man like this Man—there never has been such another. A prophet and teacher who never nagged them, never flattered or coaxed or patronized; who never made arch jokes about them, never treated them as "The women, God help us!" or "The ladies, God bless them!"; who rebuked without querulousness and praised without condescension; who took their questions and arguments seriously; who never mapped out their sphere for them, never urged them to be feminine or jeered at them for being female; who had no axe to grind and no uneasy male dignity to defend; who took them as he found them and was completely unselfconscious.[8]

Prayer

Jesus, thank You! Because of You, I have significance. Because of You, I am not defined by the world's estimation of women. Because of You, I no longer need to bear the burden I've been carrying. Help me let go of it today. I want to experience the same meaning You gave to the women You encountered as You walked this earth. Help me believe the truth You so beautifully revealed to them—that I am significant simply because You make me so. Forgive me for believing lies opposed to Your truth. Change me now through the power of Your love. Amen.

Chapter 7
Empowered by the Spirit

What's not to love about receiving a gift? When someone gives you something—whether you deserve it or not—it makes you happy. (You may exclude from this sentiment the vacuum cleaner your husband gave you before he learned proper birthday gift-giving etiquette.) Whether as simple as flowers or extravagant as expensive jewelry, gifts touch our heart. They give us that warm fuzzy feeling. They tell us someone is thinking about us, cares about us, and is willing to go out of their way to make us feel special.

Each Person of the Trinity has given special gifts to us. Each is engaged in communicating and affirming the truth about your unparalleled value as a child of God. Whether male or female, wealthy or destitute, one of the "beautiful people" or homely; whether you have two legs that work or no legs that work, God values you as His precious creation. This is true whether you *feel* valuable or not. This has been true from the start, even after humanity first fell into sin.

From the beginning, God—the one true God in three Persons: Father, Son, and Holy Spirit—in a united way has been going to great lengths to communicate your incredible worth to you. As Father, He meets your core need for love. As Son, He satisfies your need for significance. Do you receive these gifts? They are yours if you will accept them. And the Holy Spirit has more gifts for you. Important gifts. Without the Holy Spirit, not all of your needs would be met.

Who Is the Holy Spirit?

This third Person of the Trinity has a two-word name that is more mysterious to us than "Father" or "Son." In the Scriptures God is anthropomorphized, meaning He takes on human qualities and characteristics when He is described as our Father. And when we encounter Him in the Person of Jesus Christ we see Him doing all of the things we do—eating, laughing, talking, crying, touching. We can understand Father and Son because we ourselves are human beings. But the Holy Spirit is different.

The words *ruah* and *pneuma* are, respectively, Hebrew and Greek words for *spirit*. They are used "to describe and explain the experience of divine power working in, upon, around men, and understood by them as the power of God."[1] The Holy Spirit is not just a breeze or wind, though John 3:8 points out their similarities. Just as wind can seemingly come from out of nowhere, and is invisible but leaves a visible impact, so too is the Holy Spirit gentle and powerful, quiet yet unmistakable. He is Spirit. He is God's power. And He is a Person.

Jesus said, "When the Counselor comes, whom I will send to you from the Father, the Spirit of truth who goes out from the Father, he will testify about me" (John 15:26). Jesus refers to the Holy Spirit as a Person. He doesn't refer to Him as an "it." The Holy Spirit is a counselor. He is the Spirit of truth. And He comes from, or proceeds from, the Father.

Since the beginning, He has been a part of the Trinity's activity in helping us know our value. "In the beginning God created the heavens and the earth … and the Spirit of God was hovering over the waters" (Gen. 1:1–2). This is referring to the Holy Spirit. He was there; He is One of the Three! And it's through this third Person of the Trinity that your yearning for competence is filled.

Competence? you ask. *What does competence have to do with my value?* A lot, actually. It is, in fact, the third of three core human needs as noted by psychologists. We need to be loved, feel significant, and possess competence. Consider the definition of competence: "possession of required skill, knowledge, qualification, or capacity." Also, "sufficiency; a sufficient quantity," and "the quality of being competent."[2] When someone is competent, she is properly qualified for a specific role or purpose.

Can you imagine paying a pastry chef to file your taxes? I hope not. Instead, you would go to her for your best friend's birthday party, and to an accountant to have your taxes done. The first is competent in creating sweet delicacies, the other in mathematics and accounting. That's what competence is—possessing the proper skills, knowledge, qualifications, and capacity to fulfill a specific role. The Holy Spirit is the One who empowers you with competence to fulfill God's purpose for you!

The Holy Spirit is gentle
and powerful, quiet
yet unmistakable.

Yes, you have a unique-to-you calling from God. He brought you into existence for a reason. He has assigned specific purposes for your life (something we will examine in further depth in Part Three of this book), and He would not leave you improperly equipped to accomplish them. So, to bridge the gap between *you* and the fulfillment of His purposes *for* you, He grants you competence through His Holy Spirit.

Without competence you cannot effectively move forward in your unique calling. It is impossible to get something done without the competence to do it. When you lack competence, you lack know-how. If your need for competence is not met, you lack confidence. Your self-esteem tosses and turns, going up and down and all around like a leaf in a brewing storm. You feel good for a moment, and crash the next. "The heart is deceitful above all things and beyond cure. Who can understand it?" (Jer. 17:9).

When we trust in ourselves or count only on our own understanding of things, we usually mistake our limited perception for reality, instead of seeing the one true reality, which is God's truth. But when we seek guidance from the Holy Spirit, who is Himself the Spirit of truth, we receive the clarity we need.

"Not that we are competent in ourselves to claim anything for ourselves, but *our competence comes from God. He has made us competent* as ministers of a new covenant—not of the letter but of the Spirit; for the letter kills, but the Spirit gives life" (2 Cor. 3:5–6, emphasis mine). You, woman, have been given a tremendous gift by the Holy Spirit. His gift of competence is constant. If ever you doubt that, think about the round-the-clock reliability of the Holy Spirit.

The Holy Spirit's Presence

The Holy Spirit, like a perfume we cannot see but certainly sense, is sweet and desirable. His always-guaranteed, without fail, and constant presence is foundational to accepting yourself *as He made you*. If an accurate picture of your true identity is starting to make sense in your head but you're struggling to embrace it in your heart of hearts, call upon the Holy Spirit. Through His ministry of presence He will help you.

He is with you all the time, everywhere. When Jesus was preparing His disciples for the time He would be arrested and crucified, He told them, "And I will ask the Father, and he will give you another Counselor to be with you forever—the Spirit of truth. The world cannot accept him, because it neither sees him nor knows him. But you know him, for *he lives with you* and *will be in you*" (John 14:16–17, emphasis mine). Jesus assured them He would never leave them "as orphans" (John 14:18). Even though He was leaving physically, He would be with and in them through the Counselor—the Holy Spirit. Imagine that! The Holy Spirit is much closer than *next* to you; He lives *in* you!

Think about the power of another's presence. When a friend of mine suddenly lost her son in a tragic accident, I felt compelled to go visit her. If you can imagine the horror of a policeman waking you in the middle of the night to tell you that you lost a child, you can imagine stepping into my friend's world. That is exactly how she received the news. She was heartbroken.

As others stepped in to take care of her and her husband's practical needs by helping with funeral arrangements, meals, and other necessary tasks, I felt prompted to just be with them. There's not really much to say to help someone in the midst of a tidal wave of devastation. But I wanted to help. So I came and sat in their kitchen while they went about getting things done. I was just there in case they needed me. Later on, my friend told me how much that meant to her.

The same holds true when you have a sick child. You may give them medicine, plump their pillow, or refill their cup with juice, but most of the time you will simply hold them or sit with them. The ministry of presence is comforting to people, particularly when they're hurting. It communicates love and significance. Knowing that someone deems us worthy of their time builds our sense of value.

This is what God does for you. The Holy Spirit, the Person of the Trinity "whom the Scripture most often represents as being *present* to do God's work in the world,"[3] builds you up inside, brick by brick, to fill every hole of emptiness within you. The very fact of His presence is healing power for the tattered soul. Is there a greater love? Beyond salvation, is there a greater gift? Think about it—God the Spirit cares enough for you that He wants to be with you no matter what, day or night, in good times and bad. He is with you … by His own choosing! You experience Him in sweet times of worship, in everyday mundane routines, and even in the middle of unspeakable heartbreak. He is ministering to your innermost parts.

With the Holy Spirit, we are never really alone. While we are certainly called to live in community, we cannot substitute human presence for this sweet presence of God. A friend of mine who is single confesses that she does not seek a husband as desperately as some of her non-Christian single friends do. Those who do not have the Holy Spirit truly are alone. They yearn for and cling to any form of human partnership, even if it's not a healthy one. My friend says that while of course she would love to have a husband, a real person by her side, her single life is rich because of the companionship of the Holy Spirit.

The Holy Spirit Empowers You

The Holy Spirit is ever-present within you—and every brother and sister in Christ—so that among other things you may be competent to fulfill His purpose for your life. Through the Holy Spirit's ministry of presence, you are empowered to live a life of significance that profoundly impacts the world for His glory. Have you ever considered yourself to be *empowered?* Thanks to the Holy Spirit, you are!

Someone who is empowered is someone with authority. A

teacher can discipline her students because her position *empowers* her to do so. A judge can issue a sentence because her position *empowers* her to do so. Empowerment is desirable. The dictionary definition of *empower* is "to give power or authority to; to authorize." It can also mean "to enable or permit."[4] When you are empowered, you are *enabled* or *permitted* to do that which your ministry or role requires of you.

The Holy Spirit's empowering of you happened when you put your faith in Christ. You were likely not aware of this the moment you were "born again." At the time, most of us have no idea that there is even a term for such a moment! But there is (John 3:3–7). And from that time, the Spirit has been with you. You were enabled to live a godly and powerful life right then and there, and you have been empowered ever since. His empowering has likely blessed you in many awesome, specific, and tangible ways.

The Bible says, "The Spirit searches all things, even the deep things of God. For who among men knows the thoughts of a man except the man's spirit within him? In the same way no one knows the thoughts of God except the Spirit of God" (1 Cor. 2:10–11). I like that about the Holy Spirit. He goes where I cannot. He comprehends things I cannot. He does things I cannot. But when it comes to the things I need to do, He equips me to do them.

If you've been walking with the Lord for any bit of time, you know it's not the Holy Spirit's role to make everything in your life go smoothly. We still live in a fallen world where sin and its consequences are experienced. Though the Holy Spirit empowers you supernaturally, you have also been given the choice of whether or not you will listen to Him and follow Him.

"So I say, live by the Spirit, and you will not gratify the desires of the sinful nature. For the sinful nature desires what is contrary to the Spirit, and the Spirit what is contrary to the sinful nature. They are in conflict with each other, so that you do not do what you want" (Gal. 5:16–17). The spiritual battle rages and you are not exempt from it. In fact, you *are* the very battlefield in which the war is taking place.

If you are led by the Spirit, you are not following the sinful nature. If you are following the sinful nature, you are neglecting the Holy Spirit. The Bible implores us to live in such a way that we "do not grieve the Holy Spirit of God, with whom you were sealed for the day of redemption" (Eph. 4:30). We grieve Him when we ignore Him.

Of course you will make mistakes, as we all do. But my hope is that the period of time before you confess your sin is short. The Holy Spirit is your friend. He will guide you along God's chosen path for you … if you let Him. But if you neglect Him, just like a human friend, you will feel pain and remorse for doing so. And when you honor and delight Him, as with a human friend, *you* in turn experience the blessing.

The Holy Spirit's empowerment can be surprising, and that in itself is a reminder that it's not *you* at all! When He calls to your mind just the right verse to help you withstand temptation or motivate you when you are struggling against sin, that's not your doing. It's His! This is a great mystery—the combination of God's Word and the Holy Spirit. It's not something to be logically figured out. It is simply a gift to behold, accept, and utilize.

The Holy Spirit is also empowering you in ways that might escape your conscious awareness. Think about your prayer life. I don't know how often you pray, or for how long. I don't know if you are formal and regimented, or if you are casual and random. Prayer is a fascinating honor that God has given us. I am by no means an expert. But I do know that the Holy Spirit plays a critical part in our prayer life; He empowers our prayers!

> You *are* the very battlefield in which the war is taking place.

When you pray, it's His role to intercede on your behalf in accordance with God's will. "We do not know what we ought to pray for, but the Spirit himself intercedes for us with groans that words cannot express" (Rom. 8:26). I love that! Let this verse give you assurance and confidence in your prayer life. Even when you don't understand yourself, the Holy Spirit knows your heart and is at work communicating it to God.

We all have (or will have) times when we are so wrought with pain that we cannot find the words to express the depth of our suffering. We also have times of thankfulness beyond comprehension that leave us incapable of adequately expressing our gratitude. And still other times we are just "blah" and don't know how to ask God to revive us. All of this is covered by the Holy Spirit. He knows your heart and what you need to express. And He literally interprets your prayers to the Father.

Romans 8:27 says, "The Spirit intercedes for the saints in accordance with God's will." This is encouraging because it means that if our heartfelt cries are not in line with God's will, we have an Advocate who is working on the sidelines, doing a little intervention. You could think of the Spirit as a sign language interpreter. While of course God hears our original voice and requests, He comprehends them according to the Holy Spirit's interpretation.

The empowering work of the Holy Spirit is not only a privilege to experience; it is a miracle to behold. Think about what it's like to walk into your house after it has been cleaned from top to bottom … by someone *other* than yourself. I vividly remember when this happened for me as a child. Though I never saw her cleaning while I was away at school, I witnessed the work of my mom's hands everywhere when I came home. Her presence was evidenced in the dusted living room, the scrubbed sinks and showers, a fresh clean scent, and my tidied bedroom. In the same way, while we are busy doing life, the Holy Spirit is producing His fruit in us (if we are willing and cooperating, of course). The proof is in our growing spirit of love and joy, peace and patience. A life empowered by the invisible Holy Spirit is evidenced by His visible fruit (Gal. 5:22–23).

But fruit in a bowl that merely sits there looking pretty doesn't do a whole lot of good. God desires fruit in our lives for a much more practical purpose. It's through the fruit of the Spirit that we serve the Father and bless those around us. It is the fruit of the Spirit that *forms* our competence.

Did you catch that? There's a reason the Holy Spirit is with you. There is a reason He is equipping and empowering you with competence. This reason is your purpose in life. What good is it to be empowered if you don't have a role to fulfill that requires empowerment?

Jesus explicitly told us what we are called to do with our lives. He says we are to "'love the Lord your God with all your heart and with all your soul and with all your mind.' This is the first and greatest commandment. And the second is like it: 'Love your neighbor as yourself'" (Matt. 22:37–39). When you wonder why on earth you're here, God responds, "To love." And while that may sound easy enough, in all practicality, love isn't love until it is demonstrated. And love shows itself in action, through service. "This is love: not that we loved God, but that he loved us and sent [action] his Son as an atoning sacrifice [service] for our sins. Dear friends, since God so loved us, we also ought to love one another" (1 John 4:10–11).

A life of loving and serving God and others is a maximized life, a fulfilled life. Yes, you, woman, are called to a life of service. This is what you were made for! (We will more closely examine this truth in Part Three of this book.) What's more, you are not expected to draw upon your own strength to meet this calling; you are not left to pursue this life of servanthood on your own. That's why you have the empowering work of the Holy Spirit in your favor! Because even with all the incredible things the Holy Spirit does in your life, none of it would be complete without the specific spiritual gift(s) He gives you.

Empowering You with Gifts

Some gifts are purely sentimental; others are thoughtfully practical. Think of giving a photographer friend a new tripod so he can enhance his hobby. Or maybe you would give a special flower bulb to a gardener friend so she could nurture it into a beautiful plant. Both are practical gifts that also show thoughtfulness because you know they care about their crafts. In the same way, the Holy Spirit gives gifts that are both thoughtful and practical in nature. These are called "spiritual gifts."

There is much talk and, unfortunately, much confusion in Christian circles regarding spiritual gifts. But the subject matter really is quite simple, straightforward, and exciting! Spiritual gifting is a supernaturally empowered capacity to engage in one or more activities in such a way that God is glorified and the Body of Christ is built up. You'll find evidence for this definition in Scripture, which is our source of information on the matter. (Check out Romans 12, 1 Corinthians 12 and 14, Ephesians 4, and 1 Peter 4.)

The Bible tells us that the Holy Spirit dispenses gifts as He determines. It is a little bit like celebrating Christmas as a child—Mom and Dad picked out just the gifts they wanted for you, and just the gifts they wanted for your little sister Susie. You had no say in the matter. "But each man has his own gift from God; one has this gift, another has that" (1 Cor. 7:7). In other words, there is no need to look around and envy someone else's gift and devalue your own. Our response is to graciously accept and rejoice in our own gifts! A critical part of embracing your unique identity is accepting and appreciating the spiritual gifting given to you, and not fretting over that which you do not have.

Through the fruit of the Spirit,
we serve the Father and bless
those around us.

This is easier to do when we realize that spiritual gifts are not for personal gain. Rather, they are for the common good—to edify and encourage one another. You are empowered by the Holy Spirit to live a godly life and to bless others. "Each one should use whatever gift he has received to serve others, faithfully administering God's grace in its various forms" (1 Pet. 4:10).

So, what exactly are these gifts? The New Testament lists twenty of them specifically, including teaching, leading, serving, and prophesying. In the remainder of this chapter, we'll see in general terms the role our spiritual gifts play as we live out our identity as God designed us to. Although it is of paramount importance for you to not be ignorant of your gifts as you progress on this journey of discovering and embracing who God made you to be, it is beyond the scope of this book to delve into each of the specific spiritual gifts mentioned in the Bible. For that purpose, I've included additional resources in the back of the book. Appendix 2, "Spiritual Gifts and Definitions," contains two charts showing the gifts listed in Scripture and a list of definitions for the gifts. Appendix 3, "Recommended Reading," includes a list of books and online resources that will help you discover what spiritual gifts God has given you. Please take the time to go through some of them. You will not regret doing so as you learn how God has uniquely equipped you to fulfill His purpose for your life.

But as to the twenty gifts specifically mentioned in the New Testament, I don't think those twenty form a comprehensive list. The Bible never indicates that these are all of the gifts, and that outside of them there are no others. Rather, it leaves the topic open-ended and a bit of a mystery. It also doesn't say how many gifts any one person may have. I think that's because God knows how we like to put people in boxes. We like to say, "She's a teacher, so don't ask her to serve." Or, "He has the gift of prophecy, and that's all we can expect from him!" We can't do that because God is bigger than our boxes. He leaves the issue a bit mysterious.

There is wisdom in not knowing exactly how the Spirit is working in this regard. We simply need to understand spiritual gifts to the best of our ability. As Paul said, "Now about spiritual gifts, brothers, I do not want you to be ignorant" (1 Cor. 12:1). Our ignorance on the matter is what leads to confusion and misinformation. So first of all, it helps to know what distinguishes a spiritual gift from a natural talent or a fruit of the Spirit.

You are a combination of all three. You have been given spiritual gifts and natural talents, and fruit of the Spirit are growing in you. To distinguish them, think again of the definition of a spiritual gift: a *supernaturally* empowered capacity. Natural talents, on the other hand, are innate abilities given to all people at birth regardless of spiritual condition. Everyone is born with talents.

In my case, God gave me a natural ability to verbally communicate. More than thirty years ago, Fred and I were trying to figure out what to do with our lives. Neither of us knew the Lord at that point. Fred asked me, "What do you really, really like to do?" My answer was, "I really, really like to talk!" And he said, "Okay, how can you make a living talking?"

A natural communication talent was there, and I wanted to use it for my enjoyment. In college I had a radio program and was a theatre major for a while. I could talk and talk and talk! I dreamed of becoming a TV talk show host. But when I became a Christian, just as the Bible says, all things became new and the old passed away (2 Cor. 5:17). I certainly could have pursued my original dream, but my motives and desires changed. I discovered I wanted to use my talking talent for God's glory.

A nonbeliever doesn't want to maximize her talents for God's glory. She may have good intentions, but they don't involve glorifying God. And that is legitimate because she has not surrendered her life to Him who is greater than herself. Prior to becoming a Christian, I wanted to express myself, feel good, and get attention. As a theatre major I experienced the natural high that accompanies a performance. But it was always followed by a deep emptiness. Most actors and actresses need to have the next performance, like a drug fix, to feel good again. They use their talent from one show to the next, but they never fill their core need for competence. This need is something only the Holy Spirit can meet.

When a believer assesses her natural talents, she is looking to use them to serve God and others. Feeling good about herself is a nice by-product, but it is not the sole purpose for expressing her natural talents. For the believer, talents can complement spiritual gifting. They may even be empowered by the Holy Spirit to become a spiritual gift. On the other hand, they can also inhibit spiritual gifts if they're not utilized or developed. I have the spiritual gift of teaching. I also have natural verbal skills and a natural ability to persuade people. (This is one reason I love to hold garage sales … I love to convince people of the value of something I used to enjoy.) If I were unwilling to make the effort to develop my public speaking ability, or did not take the risk of standing in a classroom of adults and learning some teaching skills, my spiritual gift of teaching would be hindered from being fully expressed. But neither talents nor spiritual gifts are to be confused with fruit of the Spirit.

The fruit of the Spirit are godly character qualities listed in Galatians 5:22–23. They go with you no matter what your natural talents or spiritual gifts. A television news anchor may use her natural talent and love for speaking, but if she isn't a believer, the fruit of the Spirit will not be growing in her as it would in a believer. As you develop in your walk with the Lord and pursue a Spirit-filled life, your fruit will grow, ripen, and enhance not only who you are but all you do.

This brings us back to spiritual gifts. Again, these are supernaturally empowered capacities. Spiritual gifts are not necessarily related to positions or tasks you perform. They can be, but they may not be. And you *do* have one, if not a few. *All* believers are called and gifted by God. No one can complain that she doesn't have at least one spiritual gift. You may not know yet what it is, but you have been given at least one. But you are meant to know what it is. And you are meant to develop and use it.

But why? What is the purpose for spiritual gifts in addition to natural talent and spiritual fruit? They are uniquely given that out of your love for God you may serve Him and help build up the Body of Christ (Eph. 4:12). Again, this is part of God's purpose for you! And your service *in this way* will last for eternity! This is how you express your love. Your spiritual gift is not to be hoarded, but shared to benefit all believers (1 Cor. 12:7). It brings God great joy and it brings us great fulfillment when the Body is built up, strengthened, and matured through the use of our gifts.

In fact, it is a sin *not* to develop, steward, and invest our gifts, whether through blatant refusal or ignorant failure. Jesus teaches this in Matthew 25:14–30, when He reveals the importance of investing that which He gives us. His parable speaks in terms of money because we can grasp the concept of a monetary investment, but the principle applies to our spiritual gifts and natural talents. As you recognize your giftings, you are responsible for using them in the Body of Christ.

Through the empowering work of the Holy Spirit, you already have the competence to use your gifts. You don't have to *feel* competent. You don't have to go out and find the competence. You simply need to show up, ready and willing to be used by God. The apostle Paul exhorted Timothy not to neglect his gift (1 Tim. 4:14), and neither can we. We *must* use our gifts!

It's through the Holy Spirit that you are being shown who you really are. His empowering enables you to live it out. Scripture says God has prepared in advance good works for you to accomplish (Eph. 2:10). These are not random acts of generic kindness, but specific works prepared for you and nobody else. Your design, personality, talents, gifts, and uniqueness as an individual will work in combination to allow you to fulfill a specific role in the Body of Christ.

Now you stand at a crossroads. Your life could wither and fade away like grass. Or through the Holy Spirit's presence within you making you competent and empowering you, your life can make an eternal impact. The choice is yours. Will you do something with all He has made you to be, and all He has given you to use for His purposes? If a maximized, fulfilling life sounds like the one for you, move forward into the last part of this book. We'll look at how to break down any barriers that threaten to hinder your progress, and we'll discover how to pinpoint and take hold of your personal mandate and passion!

All believers are called
and gifted by God.

Prayer

Holy Spirit, thank You for Your ministry of presence with me. Thank You that You have made me competent for ministry and empowered me to live as You have called me. I confess the battle does rage, and I often ignore You and go my own way. I miss out on Your best for me. Help me instead to hear You and to respond to You. I praise You for the ways You have uniquely gifted me, and I ask You to help me be a wise steward of my gifts. I want my life to count for Your glory. Amen.

Part Three

Moving Forward

> *If people can't see what God is doing, they stumble all over themselves; But when they attend to what he reveals, they are most blessed.*
>
> —Proverbs 29:18 (MSG)

Having closely examined your three core needs and how each Person of the Trinity meets them, perhaps now you are wondering where to go from here. God the Father has told you how much He loves you. Jesus the Son has shown you your incredible significance, and the Holy Spirit helps you embrace this truth by empowering you with competence and spiritual gifts. Your value is imbued as an image bearer of the triune God, your Maker.

When something is imbued it is dyed, stained, or deeply penetrated. That means your value is not just a part of who you are; it *is* who you are. You cannot separate your God-given worth from yourself any more than a thread can separate its color from its fibers. If a thread is bleached white, it's not a blue thread covered in white; it's now a white thread through and through. So it is with your inherent value. It is not something you must achieve; it is a fact you must realize, accept, and live out!

Perhaps you are discovering that you have been going through life with an inaccurate view of yourself, one based on false assumptions. Maybe you're beginning to see the misconceptions and lies that have influenced you. Possibly you've leaned your ladder up against the wrong wall and climbed to the wrong destination. Now, confused about your identity, you ask, *Who am I* really? *Where do I go from here?*

Moving forward rooted firmly in the Trinity requires clarifying who you are and what your purpose in life is. These two issues are intertwined with your identity. When you don't understand who you are, you are hindered from expressing your God-given talents and giftings. And when your talents and gifts are not understood, service to God becomes obligatory and legalistic … a surefire way to sap all the energy and joy out of life. When you know who you are and understand and accept your unique purpose, you are motivated to serve by a love for God. Your life becomes passionate, energized, and fulfilling! You are effective. Joy and enthusiasm overflow!

Living in truth and fulfilling the calling that God has placed on your life aren't always easy. Be assured, it does take work. Barriers must be overcome, habits broken, and discoveries made as a unique-to-you passion becomes defined. The last part of this book offers guidance for this process. If you are willing to exert the effort, God guarantees that the freedom you will move into will be worth every ounce of it.

You will be fully and completely *you!* No longer a square peg trying to fit into a round hole, you will discover the intricate shape of your God-given design. The role you begin filling will perfectly match your shape. No squeezing or squishing. No banging your head against the wall. No trying to live a life that God never intended for you. You will become free to thrive in God's plan for your life as His image bearer.

As you become more and more your true, authentic self, you will see less and less of the same, "old" you. You will desire less and less of the things that fulfilled your "old purpose."

"This means that anyone who belongs to Christ has become a new person. The old life is gone; a new life has begun!" (2 Cor. 5:17, NLT).

God speaks. The *true you* beckons. An abundant life of purpose and vitality calls. It's time to answer. It's time to live the new you!

Chapter 8

Bye-Bye, Baggage

What if all of life were as easy as the conversation you have with the checkout clerk at the grocery store? (That's if you and he are both having a good day.) He asks how you're doing and you say, "Great, thanks." He asks if you found everything okay and you say, "I did, thanks." He asks if you'll pay by cash, check, or credit card, and you choose one of the three options. It's so simple! It's so easy. And afterward, you get a bag full of fresh food to show for it.

Small talk is essential in life. It's kind, considerate, and fosters rapport in relationships. It lightens our daily load. But when the daily hustle and bustle calms down and the quiet hours of the night seep in, the questions get harder. Our souls are tickled by the stark reality of complete stillness, and we face an abyss of longings that gnaw deep within our hearts. Sooner or later in every woman's life, these underlying, eternal questions beg for an answer. *Who am I? What defines me? Where am I going in life? Where do I find meaning? What is my purpose? What am I doing with the gifts and time God has given me?*

Left unanswered, these questions will haunt you. They may not repeat themselves in so many words day in and day out, but they will certainly keep you in their grip. Your life will lack direction and purpose. You will live with ongoing dissatisfaction, restlessness, and frustration because the unexamined life lacks clarity.

We all have the same number of hours in a day and only so many days on this earth. A friend of mine looks at her wall calendar every morning and imagines that the date's square is a box wrapped in ribbon. She literally pictures herself untying the bow at the start of every day. Her practice came about after being moved by Psalm 90:12, which states, "Teach us to number our days aright, that we may gain a heart of wisdom." She never wanted to let another day pass by without recognizing it for the gift that it is … that it's a limited resource. Our days are numbered! Her habit reminds her that she has the opportunity to either be wise with the gift of that numbered day, or be wasteful of it.

How are you investing your days? I know people who rabbit-trail for years lacking focus and direction. They look back grieving with regret. Not knowing who they were, they squandered the time they were given. Avoiding these soul-searching questions will not make you any less worthwhile, but facing them will unlock the dead bolt of your life. It will swing wide the door for fresh hope, promise, and potential to rush in. When you dare take the initiative to pursue the answers, you become a wise person who "numbers her days aright."

So, just *who* ***do*** *you think you are?* As we have been examining your God-given value, I hope you see that who *you* think you are is actually not at all the question that needs to be asked. We're fickle, aren't we? Our thoughts, attitudes, and opinions are constantly changing. God never changes His mind (1 Sam. 15:29). He is steady and consistent. And He has already profoundly answered your heart's cry to know who you are. The answer is rooted in your identity as a child of God. The simple answer is that you are His beloved child! What that looks like is defined in detail throughout Scripture. (See appendix 1, "Who Am I?")

A friend of mine looks at her wall calendar every morning and imagines that the date's square is a box wrapped in ribbon.

God the Father loves you unconditionally. God the Son elevates you, granting you unparalleled significance. And God the Holy Spirit fills you with competence to accomplish the work He has set before you. These three—Father, Son, and Holy Spirit—work cohesively to communicate the one solid, unchanging, undeniable truth that you are precious and valuable. You are His, sealed for all eternity. You are called by God to reflect Him. You bear His image as no one else ever has or will. Your life is unique, and you matter. This is the liberating truth!

But how do you move into the freedom of this truth if you have grown comfortable within the confines of lies and misinformation? It's a matter of seeing yourself as God sees you. And that requires more than merely tipping your hat to God's truth. It requires life application. It requires choosing to act on what God says about you. Not until you apply truth and act on it will it move from your head into your heart and out through your life.

Embracing Your True Identity

When someone has embraced her true identity, she can begin to live out the unique calling God has placed on her life. The first step to living your calling is to internalize a biblical perspective of your identity. My hope is that you will do this in the same way you would take hold of a map in a foreign country.

Imagine never having set foot in a strange land. Everything is new. You don't recognize the language people speak, let alone know how to read it. You can't tell north from south. So how in the world would you get from point A to point B? A map or a GPS device would become your one source for even the slightest feeling of reassurance in this uncomfortable situation.

How do you move into the freedom of truth if you have grown comfortable within the confines of lies and misinformation?

Fred is not intimidated by such unfamiliarity. He loves the adventure of striking out into the unknown. His attitude is best summarized every time he exclaims with a smile on his face, "I can figure it out!" I, however, like to know where I am going. I relish the feeling of a map in my hands or the sight of a GPS device mounted on the dash of my vehicle.

Once when we were traveling together in Budapest, we needed to head out of town toward Romania. Without a GPS available, we circled the city for half an hour. When we drove past our hotel for the second time, once again at ground zero, Fred finally admitted he needed a map. Ah … direction. True direction! The map we bought was new. It was up-to-date and reliable. We could trust it. And thanks to the map—*voilà!*—we were on our way.

We clung to it because we were lost without it. And now, no matter what anyone told us, we knew the lay of the land. Should a stranger have offered directions contrary to our map, we would have smiled and said, "Thanks, but no thanks." We could confidently drown out every voice contrary to the map because we knew it was right! We could rely on it and dismiss any confusing directions offered to us by well-meaning strangers.

This is what a biblical worldview of your identity does for you. It drowns out every lie and twisting of the truth that stands opposed to God's truth. It stands secure, steady, and true while your fickle feelings, faulty assumptions, the media, poor role models, and other such worldly influences mercilessly attack it. Nothing else matters when you hold the truth in your possession. You know who you are.

Learning to see yourself as God does, like many worthwhile efforts, is easier said than done. It is not something you will be able to check off your to-do list someday. That's because it's not a task that can be accomplished once and for all. Rather, it's a journey and a process. Some women may be further along on this journey, but no one has ever crossed the finish line, not even the most humble, spiritual woman you know. We are each on a unique timetable because we are all unique individuals. Some are late bloomers, others are early bloomers, and still others are wilting and just need to rebloom.

Chairs Need Four Legs

Every day presents another chance for you to see yourself as God does. In time, like anything that requires practice, it will get easier. But it's best to understand that this *is* a daily process. With this realistic expectation, you are more likely to stay the course.

I am going to share here four specific practices that will help you do just that. These are like the four legs of a chair. Each is essential.

You would not sit in a chair if a leg was missing or damaged. All four must be intact and in good shape. These four "chair legs" must be committed to if you want to truly embrace your God-given identity and value.

Chair Leg #1: Keep an accurate view of God.
This means knowing His true character. As we have been discussing, God is not one-dimensional. He is Three in One—Father, Son, and Holy Spirit. Nurturing your relationship with Him as such will help you better understand His nature. He is worthy of your lifelong attention.

Chair Leg #2: Maintain an accurate view of yourself.
This means seeing yourself as God sees you. Read the list in appendix 1. This is the truth about who you are. You are His image bearer. You are His precious child. There's no one like you, and you are like no one else. Because God has already met your needs for love, significance, and competence, you are free from trying to meet those needs in all the wrong places. You are free instead to pursue His specific calling on your life and to impact the world around you.

Chair Leg #3: Renew your mind.
This happens through the Holy Spirit and the reading of God's Word (1 Cor. 2:10–12; Rom. 12:2). Without these, we often unknowingly submit to such western cultural icons as independence and logic, where "knowledge is everything" and "anything goes." In other cultures we may blindly submit to such wrong ideas as "women can't/shouldn't think," and "women are not worthy." These philosophies oppose biblical thinking and wisdom. Scripture and

the Spirit reveal God's truth, and God's truth stands completely upside down from the world's way of thinking. Failing to renew your mind with His truth will cause you to backtrack on your journey to becoming all God created you to be.

Chair Leg #4: Respond to God's call.
This requires active listening on your part. It is most often in solitude and quiet that God speaks to us in our heart of hearts. An unfailing biblical principle encourages us to delight in *Him* (Ps. 37:4) … not in what He can do *for* us. As we do so, He molds our desires into *His* desires for us! We're often so close to Him at that point that we don't even recognize this change. He works to see that the real you develops, for He has your best interest in mind. Will you listen for Him? And will you respond by stewarding the gifts and talents He has given you?

Revamping your understanding of your value and identity is no small feat. Replacing an inaccurate but lifelong view of yourself with the reality of God's truth is a tremendous undertaking that may just make you want to give up before you begin. Or, what if you begin but later become *stuck?* What if you try and try to do all the right things to really make progress … but nothing seems to change?

Unpacking Your Suitcase

When you're in the thick of struggle it can feel like something vague and mysterious is holding you back. But that is usually not the reality. Your obstacles have names. We can liken them to extra weight in your suitcase. This excess weight keeps you from checking your bags at the airport unless you pay a high price for overweight baggage. If you don't pay the price, you can't move on. Here I will bring to light four specific, tangible obstacles that you need to get rid of because they will hinder you from accepting and internalizing your true identity.

Obstacle #1: Living apart from God

This is the biggest of these four obstacles. Nonbelievers have a huge disadvantage because they do not know their Creator, the very source of their identity. The only message they hear is the world's, which, as we have been learning, adamantly opposes God's truth. It screams that women are insignificant, incompetent, and not lovable. It says they are "less than," if not completely worthless.

If one does not know Jesus Christ, or keeps Him at a distance, He makes it clear that a full life will be impossible. "I am the vine; you are the branches," He says. "If a man remains in me and I in him, he will bear much fruit; *apart from me you can do nothing*" (John 15:5, emphasis mine). As believers, we must choose to remain in Him by abiding in Him. *Abiding* means being permeated through and through with Christ, our source of truth and life. Refusing to believe the world's lies is an act of obedience. It takes a bold step of faith to face a lie and say, "That is not true. I am deciding to believe the truth."

Obstacle #2: Carrying emotional, intellectual, and spiritual baggage

We all carry a lot of baggage. Imagine yourself carrying a suitcase crammed full and far exceeding the weight limit imposed by your favorite airline. You take this suitcase with you everywhere on your trip through life. It is stuffed with unmet expectations, hurts, fears, broken dreams, disappointments, failed relationships, poor parental upbringing … you name it. These things from your past will stand as roadblocks to your future as a woman emboldened by the internalized truth of her God-given identity.

It's okay and healthy to acknowledge spiritual baggage in particular. A few women in my classes have expressed how growing up in legalistic churches has weighed them down. One said, "I had to earn grace." Now, how backward is that? But unfortunately, "earning grace" is a reality for many women. Grace by definition cannot be earned. But maybe you know nothing other than always trying to measure up, trying to earn approval and acceptance. It's a difficult struggle. But it is something tangible, like an item in a suitcase that you *can* refuse to carry.

Other emotional baggage comes in the form of faulty assumptions (see chapter 2). When we wrongly assume things about ourselves, we miss out on reality. I grew up believing I should be seen and not heard. I internalized a wrong belief that I had nothing of significance to say. Years later when I took a spiritual gifts inventory as a new Christian, it identified that I had speaking gifts, including the gifts of exhortation and teaching. These results flew in the face of my "reality," so I did not respond. My incorrect assumptions about myself rang far more true to me.

Later on, when I was asked to do some teaching, different people began challenging me to attend seminary. I tentatively put out my feelers in that direction and was quite nervous, not at all convinced it was the route for me. One day a friend asked me at lunch, "Do I need to hold a mirror up to you?" I was confused. I thought I had spinach in my teeth. But of course what she meant was, "Let me show you what I see in you." She clearly saw me as a gifted teacher, and that baffled me. I just didn't see it. My wrong assumption, formed from the time I was a child and carried with me ever since, nearly kept me from fulfilling God's call on my life. Don't let that happen to you. Purposefully seek godly counsel and wise insight. Ask others to hold a mirror up to you.

> If you can pinpoint the "dirty laundry" in your luggage, you can refuse to carry it.

Obstacle #3: Allowing sin to cloud the mind

Each and every one of us shares this skewed-thinking problem (Rom. 3:12). We can thank Adam and Eve for that. While God has given each of us a mind, we treat it like we are helpless to its whims, as though we can't help the thoughts that come to us. But we *can* use our minds to control our minds. The truth is, we can use our gray matter in our favor! (See Philippians 4:8–9.) When our minds are *for* us and not *against* us, we have incredible power. But instead, we battle things like believing lies, letting others' opinions control us, and habitual low self-esteem.

If you have chronic low self-esteem, I need to tell you that you are most likely chronically self-absorbed. Women with low self-esteem are as self-absorbed as the biggest egomaniac because their thoughts revolve around themselves, their problems, and how bad or unworthy they are. This will hold you back from accomplishing anything. You won't step out in faith to do something because you will be held back by your own thoughts—the belief that you cannot do it.

Our minds are the breeding ground for fear. We fear change, failure, others' opinions, and sometimes even success. Many women have as much fear of being successful as they do of failing. Being successful just might disprove our long-held and inaccurate assumptions about ourselves!

Obstacle #4: Maintaining a temporal rather than an eternal perspective

A temporal perspective causes us to get caught up in our circumstances and robs us of seeing the big picture. When we fail to see things from God's point of view, issues that are here today and gone tomorrow consume us. We easily become anxious and sidetracked. Some common examples of the setbacks you will encounter with a temporal perspective include codependent relationships, laziness, a refusal to surrender to God, just plain disliking your gifts and talents, and lacking self-awareness.

Codependency means you are absorbed with another person and their issues to such a degree that your identity is submerged in an unhealthy way into theirs. You don't take responsibility for stewarding your gifts. You neglect finding and fulfilling God's call on your life because you are so consumed by this relationship. Instead of according God His rightful place as Lord of your life, you fill His place with another human being.

When you drift lazily through life, unconcerned about living with godly purpose and passion, you fail to make a Kingdom impact. "The precious possession of a man is diligence," says Proverbs 12:27 (NASB). With diligence, the opposite of laziness, you can live a life worthy of the calling you have received (Eph. 4:1).

Another example of a temporal perspective is simply not liking the gifts God has given you. Your limited perspective causes you to miss how these gifts are a part of God's grand plan. Your own temporal opinion should fade to nothingness next to God's master plan. Lacking self-awareness and God's eternal perspective, you will likely waste a whole lot of precious time running down the wrong path. You'll subtly envy others' gifts, or you'll try to make a strength out of a nonstrength. You'll try to be the god of your own life, instead of submitting to God as Lord of your life.

Each of these four obstacles, extra weight in your suitcase, encompasses multiple barriers to embracing a biblical perspective of yourself, and each will discourage you. But if, along the way, you can pinpoint the "dirty laundry" in your luggage, you *can* refuse to carry it. That's the cool thing about a suitcase. You can specify the pieces you'd rather not haul around inside. You can, with the Holy Spirit's help, identify your smelly socks and soiled shirts and other heavy, useless stuff. And you can promptly dispose of them. The trick is not replacing them with anything other than the beautiful garments of God's truth.

Sounds good, right? Removing the obstacles, or roadblocks, to use another common analogy, along the way to embracing your true identity is exactly what you want … but is it possible?

Removing the Roadblocks

Each and every one of us lives with a perpetual tension within. While we long to have God's view of ourselves and to love ourselves as He does, our ability to do so is challenged because of sin. This tension will never just disappear, as much as you may long for it to. Instead, it's just as much a part of being alive as breathing; it is the nature of fallen humanity. Our flesh remains susceptible to lies, a faulty perspective, and wrong behavior. But praise God, He grants us competence through the Holy Spirit!

"Therefore, dear brothers and sisters, you have no obligation to do what your sinful nature urges you to do. For if you live by its dictates, you will die. But if *through the power of the Spirit* you put to death the deeds of your sinful nature, you will live. For all who are led by the Spirit of God are children of God" (Rom. 8:12–14, NLT, emphasis mine).

Read that passage carefully. Nowhere does it state that being a child of God exempts you from struggle. You may be "led by the Spirit of God," but that does not mean you walk an easy path as a result. Quite the contrary. We are clearly in a battle of flesh versus spirit, and to win we must be committed to "putting to death" our sinful nature. Killing something (such as a desire, tendency, assumption, negative behavior pattern, etc.) that is opposed to the truth that you are God's precious image bearer takes the steady aim and unshakable focus of a sharpshooter.

Removing your roadblocks will be a lifelong process. You won't be able to call up a maintenance crew to do the job for you. I want to help you, but clearly I can't do the actual work for you. I'm going to outline here some steps that will help you remove whatever stands in your way of embracing your true identity and value. It's important to recognize these steps, but remember—only you can put them into practice. You will never regret applying enthusiastic dedication and unwavering perseverance to this process. You are worth it! God thought you—the *real* you and not some wrongly conceived version of you—were worth dying for.

Roadblock Removal #1: Identify the problem you're facing.

Name the specific roadblock that's in your way. You may feel like you're facing a mountain of them. Focus on just one at a time. You can't overcome it or remove it unless you know it by name. When a doctor treats an illness, she starts by examining the patient and taking a medical history. She tries to discern the exact source of the difficulty because in order to treat it, she must know specifically what it is. Consider the common roadblocks and pieces of luggage detailed in the previous section. You may have others. The important thing is identifying the problem. Call it out. Bring it to light and acknowledge it by writing it down, saying it out loud, confessing it to God … do what you need to do to recognize it for what it is.

Name the specific roadblock that's in your way. You can't overcome it unless you know it by name.

Roadblock Removal #2: Discover God's truth.

No lie, problem, or struggle can be counteracted without the truth. Os Guinness once said, "As human beings we are by nature truth seekers; as fallen human beings we are also by nature truth twisters."[1] Without the truth of God's Word, we are likely to mislead even ourselves. Read and listen to and study the Word of God. Write the truth where you can see it plain as day.

Roadblock Removal #3: Confess your sin and receive God's grace.

This is the liberating part! Before you can ever hope to take part in reconstructive character surgery, you must experience a complete turning to God with your need for help. This is repentance—turning away from that which is contrary to God, and turning entirely to Him for help. When you don't think rightly about God, about life, or about yourself, it is sin. When you repent, you open the floodgates of His grace. He offers it in abundance. "Let us then approach the throne of grace with confidence, so that we may receive mercy and find grace to help us in our time of need" (Heb. 4:16). God's grace is there for you. It's up to you to receive it.

Roadblock Removal #4: Exercise courage to embrace God's truth.
It takes real guts to give up wrong ways of thinking. It takes bravery to believe God's Word. A million lies may surround and infiltrate you, but they will fail next to the truth. Meditate on God's truth. Memorize it, repeat it hundreds of times a day, let it penetrate and change your mind … do whatever heavy lifting is necessary.

Hebrews 12:1–3 says, "Let us throw off everything that hinders and the sin that so easily entangles, and let us run with perseverance the race marked out for us. Let us fix our eyes on Jesus, the author and perfecter of our faith … Consider him who endured such opposition from sinful men, so that you will not grow weary and lose heart."

Roadblock Removal #5: Cultivate humility.
Receiving God's grace and staying the course is made possible through a humble attitude. If I were an expert on humility I could lend you some keen insight on the matter. But I confess that I'm more familiar with the pride end of the scale. The one thing I've learned is that on my most stubborn days, when my ego has puffed me up and I find myself standing rigidly tall, I have to stop. I have to literally cease what I'm doing and refocus. Where have I been looking but inward? The moment I take my eyes off *me* and consider instead the One who endows my very significance, that's

when I begin to cultivate genuine humility. That's when I see Jesus for who He truly is and myself for who I truly am. I am nothing without Him. He is our example. He is our source of life.

Paul reminds us in Philippians 2:3–8:

> Do nothing out of selfish ambition or vain conceit, but in humility consider others better than yourselves. Each of you should look not only to your own interests, but also to the interests of others. Your attitude should be the same as that of Christ Jesus: Who, being in very nature God, did not consider equality with God something to be grasped, but made himself nothing, taking the very nature of a servant, being made in human likeness. And being found in appearance as a man, he humbled himself and became obedient to death—even death on a cross!

Roadblock Removal #6: Choose to obey, walk in the truth, and renew your mind with the Word of God.

This obedience, this dying to yourself, is where new life comes from. Just as a seed falls to the ground and sprouts up with new life when the right conditions are in place, so also will God cause new growth and life to burst forth in you. Dying to yourself is one of the miracles of a surrendered life … that by dying you find life! (See John 12:24.) You must choose to obey, to walk in the truth, and to renew your mind with the Word of God.

No matter what the specific problem you strive to overcome, the truth will never change. You bear God's image. When you continue disrespecting yourself and refuse to tackle the problem hindering you, you sin. You are disrespecting God's creation. The truth you must continually return to is that you matter and you are designed for a purpose! You are a woman with a God-given feminine nature and God-issued spiritual gifts and strengths.

Roadblock Removal #7: Enjoy the process.
Finally, keep reminding yourself: Enjoy this process. Yes, enjoy it! God keeps teaching me to treasure each day and what He has for me. Being goal oriented is fine in the sense that it gets you going and helps keep you moving in the right direction, but this is indeed a journey. And the joy of the Lord is your strength! (See Nehemiah 8:10.) It's okay that it takes time, and that sometimes you will feel like you're starting all over again. That's normal and good because, again, this is a process. Our culture influences us to think that true change can happen as quickly as a microwave dinner can be ready to eat. That is not true. In His perfect timing God will reveal new ways He wants to shape you. Through it all you must hold fast to Him. Bathe your mind in His truth, and exercise your faith.

Flexing faith muscles isn't always easy. Getting rid of misconceptions is likely to feel really uncomfortable. Applying the truth about who you are may feel downright foreign and risky, even years into the process. It may feel sometimes like you are taking a terrifying leap of faith. Do it anyway. Your past is behind you for a reason.

Become a Visionary Christian
The apostle Paul appreciated his past, but lived in the present, and thought toward the future. He was a visionary believer. You can be, too.

In the book of Philippians, Paul talks about his past. He was very aware of who he was and where he came from. But he didn't put any confidence in any of it, or what he calls his "flesh." Paul says that if anybody thinks they have reason to put confidence in the flesh, he has more. He was circumcised on the eighth day, was born into the right family, lived on the right side of the tracks, went to the right schools, belonged to the right crowd. But none of it meant anything to Paul. He recognized that whatever had been to his profit was truly a loss for the sake of Christ. While he acknowledged his past, he didn't let it hold him back.

"Not that I have … already been made perfect, but I press on to take hold of that for which Christ Jesus took hold of me. Brothers, I do not consider myself yet to have taken hold of it. But one thing I do: Forgetting what is behind and straining toward what is ahead, I press on toward the goal to win the prize for which God has called me heavenward in Christ Jesus" (Phil. 3:12–14).

We are realistic enough to know that we don't just forget our past. We live with our past. It can haunt us, but it doesn't have to. What Paul means by the word *forgetting* is that he made a conscious choice to not let the past absorb him. He refused to let it hinder his progress. He refused to be self-absorbed. While appreciating where he came from because it pointed him to his need for Christ, he chose to be unhindered by his past. He chose to live in the present and to concentrate on the future.

That's a visionary Christian. It takes understanding your identity and exercising your ability to choose. Moving on is a choice. Embracing God's truth is a choice. Becoming the woman God calls you to be is a choice. It's not enough just to want to think rightly; you have to repeatedly take steps of action and leaps of faith.

As you understand and walk in your true identity, you will experience great freedom to be yourself. You will become more and more comfortable, enabled to express your God-given design. This brings glory to God and fulfillment to you! I hope this sounds like fun to you, because I guarantee you—it is.

In His perfect timing
God will reveal new ways
He wants to shape you.

Prayer

"Gracious and loving God, you know the deep inner patterns of my life that keep me from being totally yours. You know the misformed structures of my being that hold me in bondage to something less than your high purpose for my life. You also know my reluctance to let you have your way with me in these areas. Hear the deeper cry of my heart for wholeness, and by your grace enable me to be open to your transforming presence. Lord, have mercy."[2]

—M. Robert Mulholland, Jr.

Chapter 9

Discovering Your Mandate

Embracing your true identity is exciting and liberating work! It means you are coming to know, believe, and live out your extraordinary value as a woman of God. It means you are honoring God as your Creator, standing with Him in agreement that what He has created is indeed good, valuable, and worthwhile.

Knowing and living out our identities as God's female image bearers is an honor that can be shared by women everywhere. We are all a part of this communal objective to bring God glory as children imprinted with His character. But there is no *one* way to accomplish this overarching end. Instead, we do so through means as numerous as there are individuals. The truth is, glorifying God looks different for each and every person. I love that about God! Imagine how boring it would be if He created millions of people who said and did the exact same things. Talk about a big yawn. Instead, He unleashed His creativity by creating billions of people … no two of whom are the same.

Envision a crystal prism made up of facets too numerous to count. Behold it steady and still in your mind's eye. Allow the sun to strike it, and watch countless striking rays of light explode all around. "Three dimensional" will seem too flat a description to capture the layers, depths, shapes, and colors unfolding before your eyes. Now tilt it just a smidge. Everything changes and an entirely new display of light and color bursts forth. Continue barely changing its position, and you will never see the same thing twice.

This is how it is with all the people in the world. Each person is just one facet in the gigantic prism of humanity. No two are the same. God's light shines through each of us in a unique and profound way. Put together as one Body of Christ, our inimitable contributions combine to create one magnificent image that reflects our Creator. This is an awesome and glorious picture to behold!

God has intricately fashioned the prism of humanity part by part, person by person. He does not gloss over one facet to spend more time on the next. Each is precious. Each has a distinct purpose. He made you uniquely *you* for His own special purpose. No one else can claim it. Does that get you excited? I hope so, because this truth has the power to change the trajectory of your life as you now know it.

Your Personal Mandate

God's purpose for you—and you alone—is what I call your personal mandate. Your personal mandate fits your identity as His image bearer like a glove fits a hand. They—your identity and mandate—are made for each other. Identity has to do with *who* you are, and mandate has to do with *expressing* who God made you to be. Discovering your individual mandate means discovering your unique mission in life.

Remember what I emphasized at the beginning of this book: the role or roles you play at any given time in your life do not define you. They are not *who* you are. You may be a wife or single, a mother or childless, a stay-at-home mom or a career woman, widowed or divorced, a volleyball coach or the president of the neighborhood association, a Sunday school teacher or a bank president … whatever! These roles are not *you*. They are what you do. Roles do not make you valuable. They do not define who you are. God is the One who imbues you with value.

As we have been exploring, your incontestable value and identity as a woman of God are found only in God the Father, Jesus the

Son, and the Holy Spirit. That's the hand in this hand-and-glove analogy: *who* you are as defined by the Three in One. What we will look at in this chapter is the "glove," or the *way* you express yourself to God's glory. Just remember that the glove will never be the hand. Your personal mandate (glove) expresses your identity (hand). It never *is* your identity.

As you know, you can't just try on any ol' pair of gloves and expect them to work. They may be too tight, floppy, scratchy, thick, thin, or just plain ugly for your taste unless they are gloves made specifically for your unique hands. Many of us try to fill various roles without truly understanding ourselves. We jump into things without considering our design. That's like wearing clunky mittens while you're trying to sew. It just doesn't work.

Your personal mandate fits your
identity as His image bearer
like a glove fits a hand.

Think about a "people person" who works as a computer technician or in another solitary job day in and out. Or imagine a quiet, introverted person who thrives on structure trying to teach a chaotic kindergarten class. Many roles just won't fit us. And it's not that they *should* fit us. It's that God has designed a specific mandate for you that makes sense with who He made you to be. (Note: I am not talking here about being a wife and mother. If you are married with children, it is God's will for you to be faithful and function in these roles. You are not to abandon them because you think you were not gifted with a mom's skill set. Rather, you function in that role *through* your unique personality and gifting.)

God's mandate for you is a glorious thing to take hold of, or, as this analogy would have it, to be properly fitted with. But your life will be a series of frustrating experiences much worse than trying on multiple gloves at a department store if you don't take time to do a little self-inventory.

As we saw in chapter 7, God has given you *spiritual gifts* and *natural talents.* He wants you to use these for His glory and to serve others. It's important that you discover your spiritual gifts and natural talents so that you can properly steward them. Other aspects also factor into your mandate because you are multifaceted. You are made up of many things and have many layers. You are, after all, fearfully and wonderfully made! (See Psalm 139:14.)

You have *capacities*—intellectual, physical, and emotional. You have *passions*—perhaps falling under a broad umbrella like "social" or "political," or perhaps as specific as making jewelry. (We will more closely examine passions in the last chapter.) You have a unique *personality* and a specific *temperament.* You have primary *values*—such as order, precision, flexibility, or creativity.

You have to understand who you are in order to know how and where to invest yourself. Think about money management. People who know about money and how to handle it are better investors because they understand it. The same applies to your very self. The better you know yourself, the better you'll "manage" yourself, and the greater the return will be on the investment of your life. Many books and resources exploring personality types, temperaments, and other such tools for self-discovery are available. See appendix 3, "Recommended Reading," in the back of this book for a few suggestions.

I encourage you to take the time to do a self-inventory or assessment. Among many other benefits, you will reap a clarified sense of life direction. From your daily decisions to your overall life's course, increased self-awareness of your strengths and gifts will help you know what to say yes to and what to say no to. Many women have a hard time saying no to things that come up because they think they must be available for *everything*. Greater self-knowledge and acceptance gives you greater freedom to make wise use of your time—guilt free!

If you think you are of a certain age and therefore it's unnecessary that you do a self-assessment, I encourage you to reconsider. You may know yourself, but how well? Or you may know who you were twenty years ago, but who are you today? We are always growing and changing. We need to keep up with ourselves! Taking a self-inventory is not only eye-opening, it frees you to become less judgmental.

When you know yourself well, you lighten up in your assessment of yourself and of others. We are hardest on ourselves when we think we are not measuring up to some elusive ideal (usually something that was never meant to be us in the first place). And we are hypercritical of others when they fail to fit into a mold that we wish they did. But when you understand the intricacies that make you and other individuals special, you are free to accept and even embrace your differences. This will lead to an overall improvement in your relationships. You won't put pressure on others to meet needs that they really can't meet anyway. You will understand your limits, and what needs only God can fulfill.

An accurate self-assessment helps you understand, value, and embrace your unique design. It gives you insight into God's plan for your specific contribution in life. Your individual mandate affirms your identity. It will never contradict the fact that you are God's image bearer whom He loves deeply, endows with significance, and equips with competence for His tasks. And remember, of course, that God will never call you to do something that He has not equipped you to do.

God has a specific purpose
and plan for your life!

Your Calling Is Calling

Søren Kierkegaard was a nineteenth-century Christian philosopher who said, "At each man's birth, there comes into being an eternal vocation for him, expressly for him."[1] The words *vocation* and *calling* are the same root word in Latin. Kierkegaard meant that from day one, each and every one of us is given a special, eternal purpose. (The word *man* here refers to all of humanity.) But don't just take a philosopher's word on this, take God's! "Before I formed you in the womb I knew you, before you were born I set you apart," He says in Jeremiah 1:5. Christ says in John 15:16, "You did not choose me, but I chose you and appointed you to go and bear fruit—fruit that will last." Ephesians 2:10 states, "For we are God's workmanship, created in Christ Jesus to do good works, which God prepared in advance for us to do." Scripture abounds with the truth that God has a specific purpose and plan for your life!

Consider Paul's words in Colossians 4:17, "Tell Archippus: 'See to it that you complete the work [ministry] you have received in the Lord.'" Would Paul have made such an exhortation if God did not assign specific work for specific people? Here we see that Archippus was called by God to accomplish a task, and Paul was prompting him to pursue it.

God has a unique stamp on your life and a specific work for you to do. The better you know yourself (your spiritual gifts, natural talents, temperament, personality, passions, values, etc.), the easier it will be to put the "glove" of your personal mandate on the "hand" of your identity as God's female image bearer. That's when you can really hit your stride and fulfill your calling!

Please hear me when I say that the personal mandate we are talking about here is not automatically equivalent to your day job. In America, discovering and preparing for one's line of work is emphasized to an extreme. I'm afraid it has caused most young people incredible and unnecessary stress. They think they have to find one exact career or job that is just right for them, and if they miss the bull's-eye their life will be for naught. Though this is typical thinking in America, it's simply not true. A job is what pays you. Your job may be to pick up garbage or to clean bathrooms every day. Does that mean you *are* garbage or that you are nothing more than a can of bathroom cleanser? Of course not! Again, your role or your job will never define you.

Some people are blessed to have a job or career that maximizes their giftings, capabilities, and talents. But even if the job that pays you is not the best fit for you, you can still live out your personal mandate. (Most of us need work simply to survive.) There are other ways to serve and to thrive than within the confines of a paying job. Think about positions in your church. What about in your neighborhood? Perhaps at your local public school, or in your own home. Nowhere in Colossians 4:17 does it say that this is a paid day job that Archippus needs to go out and apply for. God is much bigger than that.

Jesus taught that the first and greatest commandment is to "'Love the Lord your God with all your heart and with all your soul and with all your mind.' … The second is like it: 'Love your neighbor as yourself'" (Matt. 22:37, 39). The first and second commandments—straight from the Lord's lips—can be done anytime, anywhere, whether you have clearly defined what God would have you do or not. Paul said we should "live a life of love, just as Christ loved us and gave himself up for us" (Eph. 5:2). We can live a life of love anywhere, anytime. Our personal mandate, however different it may be from other believers', has in common with all believers this call to live a life of love, no matter what.

If you have been blessed with employment right now but you think it's not the right glove for your hand, I'm not advising you to quit and be done with it. Rather, your personal mandate is about something much bigger than a paycheck. It involves your entire life, not just your working hours. It's an opportunity for you to bring glory to God and to serve those around you. The specific way that you do so can happen at your day job, of course, or perhaps through a volunteer position. Or even through no official position at all!

I know a woman who has been a CPA (certified public accountant) for about forty of her sixty years of life. Does she think that job is her personal mandate from God? Perhaps, because she *is* good with numbers, but where she finds true joy is in leading small group Bible studies and mentoring young women one-on-one. How exciting! She knows the strengths God has given her, and she has found a perfect fit for herself in these roles that she fulfills apart from her work as an accountant. She is serving God, loving and blessing people, and thrilled with her part in it all!

With a mistaken identity, when you misunderstand or refuse to believe how much you are loved and valued by God, you might go about fulfilling your personal mandate because you think you *should*, out of obligation. That's when your behavior becomes rote or even resentful. When you're motivated, however, by the love of God the Father; when you accept and are filled with the significance and competence He grants you; when you know the intricacies of yourself—including your spiritual gifts, natural talents, personality, temperament, passion, and more; and when you're thrilled by the joy of giving it all back to Him because you love Him … that's when you will fervently and energetically serve the Lord!

Understanding your identity and value is important to discovering your mandate because it will give you joy and freedom in service. Two women with similar giftings and talents may go about exactly the same activity and have entirely different experiences. One may serve out of the overflow of God's love in her heart and the empowering of the Holy Spirit, while the other may be motivated by a sense of duty, or a sense of *I guess I* should *do this.* The first just can't seem to get enough, and the latter is resentful and irritated. Who do you think is having more fun?

Let me tell you, serving God *is* meant to be enjoyable. Many people have the false perception that living out their personal mandate is drudgery. That God requires service because He doesn't want us having any fun. Quite the contrary! When you discover how your mandate fits perfectly with your unique identity, you will hit a stride that makes loving God and serving people the most fulfilling thing you will ever do.

Fred loves to lead and serve and travel. He is a gifted cross-cultural worker. When we go on overseas ministry trips, his "ministry juices" propel him forward. He just can't help people enough (that's his serving gift). And he loves to motivate and direct people to accomplish God's purposes (that's his leadership gift). I love to teach and open minds to God's truth. I don't enjoy the travel as much as I love meeting new people and sharing God's truth in a way they can understand and apply (that's my teaching gift). Together Fred and I have a wonderful time. He appreciates that I desire to teach and need time to reflect. I release him to serve, lead, and enable people to grow. We have learned to respect our differences and enjoy the process together.

The people who serve only out of a sense of duty and obligation, and who lack joy and heart in their service, have perhaps not pinpointed their personal mandate. Or maybe they have but they've lost perspective. They've forgotten their identity as God's image bearers. They're living on the outside but dying on the inside. Those are the people who eventually give up, walk away from the Lord, or just live a very empty life.

Christ is our ultimate example of One who finished well.

I remember when a friend of mine up and left his wife one day. "This Christian life is too hard," he said. "I can't do it." He quit. He walked out. He did not understand the internal motivation and joy of loving God and walking with the Lord, or how to live out who God created him to be. He instead lived from the "outside in"—striving to do everything right on the outside, while completely lacking the internal peace that comes from a rich relationship with the triune God. It was too much of a burden for him, and he gave up.

This man tried to do it all on his own. God does not ask any of us to do that. We would all fail miserably. But because God has deposited His Holy Spirit within you, it is through *His* empowering that you can discover, seize, and fulfill your personal mandate. With God's own Son as our perfect human example, we can graciously, humbly, and *lovingly* serve Him and those around us.

I emphasize love because, ironically, it's one of the first things we can leave in the dust as we eagerly move into God's purpose for our lives. It can become all about me, instead of about living for God, our Creator. But without love we cannot reflect God, who is Himself love (1 John 4:16). Remember, discovering our personal mandate is not ultimately about self-fulfillment, but about living the life God intended for us to live. So "Let love be your highest goal" (1 Cor. 14:1, NLT) because without it, even if you are employing your spiritual gifts and expressing who you are, you will never have a Kingdom impact. Love God. Love others. Without love you will be hollow, "a noisy gong or a clanging cymbal," as Paul says in 1 Corinthians 13:1 (NLT). *With* God and with His love, your life can be all about His glory, His people, and His Kingdom. Because He fills you, you can fill others.

Four Key Life Areas

Your personal mandate is an outward expression of who God uniquely created you to be. The days of our youth are punctuated with struggle to discover and express ourselves. It can be a time of trial and error, turmoil and upset. But in time, as we mature, our vision sharpens and we begin to see ourselves for who we truly are. Discovering your personal mandate is akin to finding your voice. Living it out is like spreading your wings. You will take flight as you express your core self, the *real* you as defined by your Maker.

On your way to discovering your personal mandate, or as you live it out and refine it, I encourage you to heed four key life areas. Attending to these will help you stay the course to the end. And they are all important. Christ is our ultimate example of One who finished well. At the end of His life, He said, "It is finished" (John 19:30). He could say with a clear conscience that He accomplished what the Father sent Him to do. Can you imagine at the end of your life being able to say, "Lord, my life was an offering to you. May you find that I accomplished that which You asked me to do"?

Life Key #1: Spiritual Life

Just as Jesus took time alone to pray and be with the Father, we are wise to follow His example. Regular time spent alone with God spills over in wonderful ways to every area of life. Practicing spiritual disciplines (prayer, fellowship with other believers, Bible study, fasting, service, etc.) will help you listen to, follow, and grow in the Lord. Of course there is no formula or timetable to follow because by Christ's sacrifice we are under grace and not the law. Your faith is not about you performing or doing all the right things all the time. However, a spiritually disciplined life is a fruitful life.

A discipline is not something you do every now and then. A discipline is a habit. Research has shown that it takes twenty-eight days to establish or break a habit. If it sounds impossible to you that you would start, for example, regularly reading the Bible or praying, try giving it your all for twenty-eight solid days. After that, it will likely come easier because you have established it as a habit. Discipline is important because without it you simply won't grow. Following Jesus as His disciple means you are in relationship with Him. And that relationship, like any, takes consistent time and attention.

Life Key #2: Relational Life

What kind of people are in your life? Who fills you up? Who drains you? Romans 12:18 holds prudent counsel for us: "If it is possible, as far as it depends on you, live at peace with everyone." It's easy to live at peace with people you like, harder with the difficult people in your world. But the Scripture does say *everyone.* And it does say *"as far as it depends on you."*

To live out this passage, keep short accounts with others. We must learn to forgive and let go … again and again. Sometimes letting go means choosing new friends. Some relational problems we can correct, but there are some issues and people that, no matter how hard we try, cannot be fixed or restored.

It's a fact of life that we will have "givers" in our life and we will have "takers." On any given day you may feel like your life is unbalanced and the draining people far outnumber the fill-you-up people. Love the people who drain you, but also have appropriate boundaries so they don't control your life. It is critical that you intentionally seek out mentors, encouragers, and fellow believers who will pour into you and support you. Ecclesiastes 4:10 is a verse we can all resonate with: "If one falls down, his friend can help him up. But pity the man who falls and has no one to help him up!" We need friends along our journey. You will be wise to nurture friendships with the right people.

Joy is not a luxury; it is a necessity.

Life Key #3: Educational Life

Are your gifts underutilized or lying dormant because they require skills that you currently do not have? Do you have the give of exhortation, but don't know how to counsel? Or perhaps you have the gift of prophecy but don't know the Word of God?

Maybe you are like I was when the lightbulb in my head began to illuminate and I realized that I was made to teach. You may think of your mandate, *That can't be right. That's not me!* But sure enough, it is. The main thing standing in your way, other than accepting the surprising truth about yourself, is developing the actual skill to do it!

After finally giving up arguing with the Lord about becoming a teacher, I got to work and sought the practical training that was necessary. Though I had a natural talent for communicating and the spiritual gifts of teaching and leading, I needed to develop practical skills to express those gifts by pursuing higher education. When I did it was like a tailor had altered my clothes to fit me perfectly. No more tugging, sucking in, or stretching out. I was wearing clothes that fit my exact measurements. God knew me better than I knew myself. When I submitted to Him, accepted the discipline of higher education, and accepted myself the way He made me, my life really began. It has brought me more joy than I thought possible to fulfill His call on my life, to fulfill what God created me to do!

Maybe you're not a school or book person but you learn in other ways. Let me encourage you to always keep learning. It is a mental discipline to expand your thinking, I know. But it is crucial. It keeps your mind sharp and broadens the scope of your world. God gave you a mind and He wants you to use it. Proverbs 1:5 says, "Let the wise listen and *add to their learning,* and let the discerning *get guidance*" (emphasis mine).

Ask someone who has a job you are interested in if you can

spend a few hours observing or "job shadowing" them. Read books and materials that challenge you. Ask questions. Set goals. Start at square one and practice a skill. Improvement will come. Actively pursue an education, formal or informal, and you will never cease to be amazed … and you will become a more interesting and humble person. Lifelong learners can't help but be humble because they are always learning just how much more they have to learn!

Life Key #4: Physical and Emotional Life

Are you taking care of yourself? Often, the first thing women sacrifice in their quest to take care of others and fulfill their many responsibilities is themselves. This does more harm than good. "Do you not know that your body is a temple of the Holy Spirit, who is in you, whom you have received from God? You are not your own; you were bought at a price" (1 Cor. 6:19–20). Are you taking care of your temple?

No matter how much you have packed into your schedule, it *is* possible to strike a proper balance of physical exercise, rest, and nutrition. (Of course extreme circumstances will pose an exception to this, but on a general day-to-day basis, maintaining physical health and wellness is possible.) Lifestyle changes may be necessary, but they are doable. Jot down what you do each hour of the day for several days. This "time audit" will pinpoint where you are wasting or losing time, and it will show where you are unbalanced.

Less obvious perhaps is the necessity of your emotional health. Some bounce back from difficulties and disappointments more easily than others. Some are more easily discouraged. That has to do with our temperamental differences. Truth is, we all get weary and have times of discouragement. When you are emotionally down, it is all the more crucial for you to be spiritually revived through time with God. You need to be regularly filled and refilled with joy. Joy is not a luxury; it is a necessity. No matter how dire your circumstances, the joy of the Lord is your strength (Neh. 8:10). Spend time reflecting on your Creator. Read the Psalms. Take care of the temple (yourself). When you need to rest, rest. Setting proper boundaries that allow for emotional rest will foster your emotional stamina. It may be challenging to make time to care for yourself, but when you embrace your God-given value, you agree that you are worth it. Physical and emotional health allow you to fulfill your personal mandate with energy and gusto! This is good. This is God's design.

Tending to each of these four key life areas will bless you. It will prepare you to start *and* stay the course … the course being the journey of your *real* life—the life of Christ in you (Col. 1:27). Preparation is no easy task, and it's not for the faint of heart. But God uses prepared people. And prepared people put forth the effort. Leonard Sweet says, "Every journey begins with initiative, lots of risk, and a leap of some kind."[2]

And so I ask: are you ready to make a leap of faith and begin the journey? Being fitted with the perfect glove for your unique hand, or finding your personal mandate, is exhilarating. But there is one more crucial part of you that, understood and embraced, helps you become who God designed you to be. It is a simple thing called *passion.* Passion is a gift from God to you so that you will find much joy and great satisfaction in your personal mandate. Passion is the final ingredient that makes your mandate your sweet spot.

Prayer

Lord, thank You for making me Your child! I confess that I have not properly valued the specific ways You have made me unique, and I ask for Your forgiveness. I want to know myself well. I want to honor You with the specific ways You have gifted me and all the ways You have formed me to be who I am today. Please guide me along the process of self-discovery and make known to me what You have me here to do. I want my life to be a pleasing offering to You. Amen.

Chapter 10

Hello, Sweet Spot

What gets you out of bed in the morning? For me today it was Bailey, my dog. He saw a cat dash across the front yard, and all my dreams of a peaceful, quiet morning under the covers vanished into the thin, ruckus-filled air. Most mornings my alarm is much more gentle—it's the smell of coffee wafting in from the kitchen where my husband is already gearing up for his day. That's how I like to be awakened, lured out of bed rather than forced out.

But there's something much more powerful than these situational challenges to my slumber that gets me going every day. While I have daily responsibilities to tend to (including quieting my dog), and while I do adore the smell of coffee, those really don't propel me through the day. Do you know what I mean? You may be a regular at Starbucks, but your passion for the coffee bean might as well be ground to dust and blown away when you compare it to what *truly* fires you up for living. Don't get me wrong—nothing can replace the beauty of the bean. But if you didn't have the kind of passion that makes life worth living, you would likely crawl right back into bed after your cup of joe.

Please do feel free to grab your favorite cuppa goodness and enjoy it as you finish this book. The kind of passion we're going to be talking about in this chapter is not the kind that wears off like your morning coffee. It will stick with you long after your brief caffeine pick-me-up lets you down. Temporary things may inspire you out of bed every morning, but they won't get you through the day. They won't bring life to your bones, let alone change your life as you know it. A God-sized passion, however, most certainly will.

What Is Passion?

The definition of *passion* as I mean it in this chapter is a deep-seated, enthusiastic, can't-ignore-it desire from God to impact the world. This is no passing passion. It's not a hunger pang, a desire for coffee, or a sexual urge. Those are passions of a specific, intense feeling and emotion. The passion I'm talking about is of the kind that breeds motivation, vision, hopes, and dreams. It is not itself an emotion, though it is marked by such. You can't have this passion without knowing it by the zeal it makes you feel.

Philippians 2:13 says, "It is *God* who works in you to will and to act according to his good purpose" (emphasis mine). He is the very source of this passion! When God is working in and through you, *His* dreams are placed in your heart so that you will discover, embrace, pursue, and fulfill them.

Would God make you a flat plate if He wanted you to be a vessel that transports water? No. Would He make you a chair if He wanted you to display books? Likely not. Or would He make you a cup of espresso if His intent was for you to mellow people out? Certainly not! You see, your passion connects with your personality, character, and intricate design. It fits your giftings. It does not contradict them. Your passion actually fits *you* perfectly. God is a wise, brilliant, and orderly Creator. He did not haphazardly put you together with random giftings, talents, personality, temperament, capacities, and values. He intentionally crafted you and equipped you to fulfill the very passion that He has set within your heart.

Without this passion, you may do all the hard work of overcoming your roadblocks to embrace your inherent value, to know who you are, define your giftings, and so forth, but you may never be motivated to live out God's calling on your life. Without passion you will lack the inner motivation to get going, and to keep going for the long haul. Without passion, you may look back a year or two or twenty from now on your experience reading this book and say, "Sure, it was helpful to learn how God sees me and created me as unique, but that was then. Now I'm just living. I put one foot in front of the other. *Ho hum.*" It is quite likely you could end up very, very bored.

Without passion, you may be driven but joyless. Being driven is highly valued in America and other cold-climate countries. Calling someone driven in the corporate world is considered a compliment because drive is associated with success. Do you know any driven people? A friend of mine embodies what it is to be driven. She is intensely focused, determined, and resolute. Driven people know where they're going, they have a plan for getting there, and they refuse to be sidetracked by any distraction.

However, that kind of drive is not what I mean when I talk about the passion planted in you by the indwelling Holy Spirit. A driven person who is not motivated by godly passion is enslaved. She works out of a compulsive sense of obligation. When you are so focused on a goal that the process of getting there is more about you and your achievement, you fail to enjoy the journey. The good news is that God will never drive you. Instead, He instills in you this passion that will compel you to godly action. You may not know yet what your passion is, but if you are a Spirit-filled Christian, it *is* in you.

With your passion, you're empowered from within to grab and hang on to a singular goal for a long time—for the rest of your life! Like a driven person, you can focus on it without wavering. But unlike a driven person, you will be internally motivated by the Holy Spirit. And His presence never fades, dwindles, or dissipates. While at times you may lose sight of your passion, through His indwelling you will be led back to it again and again. And you will experience joy and delight in the journey.

> Would God make you a flat plate if He wanted you to be a vessel that transports water? No.

Psalm 37:4 states, "Delight yourself in the LORD and He will give you the desires of your heart." I don't think the desires being referenced here are passing wants. You may want a new car, but this verse is not dishing out materialistic advice. What it means is that as you enjoy the Lord's presence and get to know Him more and more, He molds and shapes you. He changes your inner desires. He allows you to feel ownership of what are actually *His* desires for you. When you are consumed with the triune God, your passion is never selfish because His desires become your desires.

Your passion springs from God, who dwells within you. Your passion transforms the mundane-sounding "personal mandate" (the unique expression of your identity as God's image-bearing daughter) into that which it really is—your sweet spot. Without passion you have a generic mandate to love God and serve others (Mark 12:29–31). But *with* your God-given passion, your personal mandate becomes a joy, a thrill, and the adventure of a lifetime!

Discovering Your Passion

Just what is your passion? Do you know what it is? I realize I get the easy part in asking you this question. You have the challenging part of answering it. If you do know your passion, you are likely either living it out already or making strides toward doing so. Passion is not something you can ignore. It won't let you sit idly as you merely acknowledge it. Like the power of a magnet, it will attract you so that you can't help but use it to God's glory and the benefit of others.

If you don't know your passion, that's okay! Assessing your natural talents, spiritual gifts, and the many things that make you *you* will help. This will be a process, and it may not come right away. If you're just being introduced to the concept of God's passion within you and you'd like to discover it, you can pay attention to a few indicators that will help you recognize it.

First, don't underestimate the role of your life experiences. If you have many birthday candles to your credit, you have more years to draw from. If you are in your teens, you have fewer years behind you but equally important past experiences. Pay attention to where you've been and what you've been through. Take note of the highs and the lows. Ask yourself what challenges you have faced or are perhaps now facing.

Your passion may be born from a crucible. When you go through a difficult time, it can clarify what's important to you and where you want to invest yourself. Perhaps you are being molded and directed somewhere new in light of the challenges. Sometimes we resist changing our life's course when it's the result of a drawn-out period of difficulty. We just don't want to feel defeated by what's happened to us. But as with everything in our lives, God has allowed our circumstances.

I think of a friend whose adult daughter barely survived a car accident. It left her with significant physical limitations and a traumatic brain injury that put her at a child's learning level and wiped out her long-term memory. My friend gave up her career to become her daughter's full-time caregiver. In the process she has become a massage therapist and an expert on natural treatments, remedies, and supplements. She loves that stuff! In "considering it pure joy" as you face trials of many kinds (James 1:2), you allow yourself to be shaped, molded, and even to become a bigger person as a result of the crucible. You say *yes* to letting God have His way in you.

A shorter-term but just as dramatic challenge may prompt your passion. People who have survived heart attacks or near-death accidents or illnesses can have a complete turnaround in the way they invest their time. They discover a newfound, God-given direction for their lives.

Or, your passion could be born as you go about everyday living. You may experience an epiphany, or an "aha moment." This is when something triggers new insight. You could be reading a book, listening to music, watching a movie, talking with a friend, sitting in church, or doing any given standard activity when the Holy Spirit suddenly adjusts your antenna. Words may leap off the page and resonate with you. Music may become a symphony and spark in your heart a newfangled tune. Insight from a friend may make the entire world fade away as you see an old concept with twenty-twenty vision.

Aside from these periods or moments in your life, notice what you are doing or thinking about when you completely lose track of time. When you're engaged in something you love, you aren't watching the clock. Pay attention to what activities energize rather than deplete you. "Mind your mind." What mentally invigorates you? Where does your mind drift as you daydream? What do you reflect on? The things you think about are the things you value. These can be significant clues about what God has placed on your heart.

This search process may require putting yourself in different environments and trying different things. It may take trial and error. Notice your body's cues. When you get excited about something, your body responds. Your attention span increases. Your eyes get larger and your heart rate increases. Your voice may become louder or higher pitched and you might begin talking faster. Your attention focuses like a laser. You feel energized and "dialed in."

Take all of these things to the Lord. Dream with Him! Believe in God's transcendent presence and His power to invade your world, and trust His ability to fulfill His plans through you in spite of the obstacles you see. Think big! Imagine possibilities that might otherwise scare you. That's what dreams are for—they bring you outside of yourself and the confines of your rational mind. Ask the Holy Spirit to speak to your gut and to prompt your intuition. Make a pointed effort to stay in tune with Him.

My husband and I were adults before we received the gift of new life in Christ. Early in our Christian life, I felt like there was something we were supposed to do, but I had no idea what it was. We were growing and we were serving, but I just knew—through that Holy Spirit "gut sense"—that there was something else He had for us to do.

We went to seminars and conferences. We took classes. Then we adopted two boys, and that brought us a whole new set of responsibilities and demands. At that point we realized it was okay to be faithful to the tasks in front of us while continuing to grow in the Lord. It was okay to stop trying to figure it all out and simply dedicate ourselves to God, each other, and our children.

Ten years down the road, the door to seminary opened for us. Now, more than a decade later, I know with certainty that we are doing exactly what we're supposed to be doing. We are serving in our areas of passion! God replaced our uncertainty with crystal-clear, laser-sharp vision. I see now that God had other things for us to do (raising a family) before calling us into our specific areas of passion. During that preparatory season He was developing and refining our character. He was growing us spiritually before He revealed to us His next step.

Take all of these things to the Lord.
Dream with Him!

It's all in God's timing. If you are frustrated and questioning how in the world you're supposed to find your passion, don't give up. Be faithful, persistent, and observant. Keep dreaming and keep walking in what God has for you at this moment. But do fasten your seat belt, because God is a God of sudden opportunities. He is always steadily working, yet there are times when He opens doors so fast that it makes your head spin. Think about emergency medical technicians who train for life-or-death moments, yet they spend most of their time waiting to be called on. That's how it is for God's children as we anticipate His call upon our life. When the time is right and God reveals just what He has for you, may you be prepared and ready to respond! You can do that by being faithful in loving Him and loving others in simple ways. When you steward well the gifts He has given you, you prepare yourself to move forward for His glory with joy!

Obstacles to Passion

God may withhold revealing your next step for Him until your character has been further refined and matured. But when something other than His perfect timing threatens to prevent you from knowing and living out your passion (which, remember, is actually *His* passion), you must do all you can to overcome that obstacle. First Peter 5:8 encourages us to "be self-controlled and alert. Your enemy the devil prowls around like a roaring lion looking for someone to devour." That *someone* is you.

Satan does not play fair. He will use anything he can to defeat or at least distract you from the abundant life God has for you. He will use baggage from your past. He will use unresolved emotional damage. He will use the same old lies you have long believed. Don't let him win. You must fight back. Use the tools in chapter 8 for unpacking your baggage and removing roadblocks. Defend yourself against his attacks so that you do not become dull, hindered, and void of the passion God longs for you to grow into. Commit to being "strong in the Lord and in his mighty power" (Eph. 6:10).

Of course life challenges and crises may drain and exhaust you. You may become dried out, disillusioned, defeated, or disheartened at any time. If any of those states are prolonged, it will rob you of your enthusiasm and tempt you to wallow in doubt, negativity, despair, and loneliness. There are many individuals in the Bible who struggled with these feelings and lost their original God-given passion. They had to have it revived, some more than once. But revived it was, because new life is God's specialty!

Just don't let fear shut you down, because it will keep you from this new life. When you are afraid to dream, are timid to express your heart, or dread failure, you will freeze in a state of inactivity. You won't be able to thaw, let alone feel the burn of passion. If satisfying or impressing others has become more important to you than pleasing God, now is the time to kiss your fear of rejection good-bye. Embracing God's call on your life and pursuing it with godly enthusiasm is thrilling, like winning the million-dollar lottery. Winning is when you find and move into the joy of your own God-granted passion.

When I started seminary in my forties, I had to face some naysayers in my life. (But not Fred. He has always encouraged my growth and development.) I received comments—even from people I knew well and loved dearly—along the lines of, "Well, why would you want to do that at this time in your life?" People were truly puzzled as to why I would do something outside the norm. Comments like that will feed your sense of insecurity and make you think, *Maybe I'm not doing the right thing. Maybe I'm not smart enough. Maybe I am the wrong gender. Maybe this isn't really God's idea.* The negative messages will play over and over. They will hold you in bondage.

It's just like Satan to disguise a tissue paper–thin fear as an insurmountable brick wall.

But those comments and thoughts are really just that—voices, mental recordings, and threats to faithful living. They are not actual obstacles. Have you heard the saying that fear is only paper thin? Picture a piece of tissue paper. What if the one thing standing between you and your heart's passion was literally a piece of tissue paper? The moment you realized it held no real power over you, wouldn't you laugh and run right through it like a little girl bursting through a lawn sprinkler on a hot summer day?

It takes courage to run through the obstacles Satan will toss in your path. It's just like him to disguise a tissue paper–thin fear as an insurmountable brick wall. The questions you must pointedly return to are, *If no one was judging me, what would I do? If it was just God and me, and He equipped me with everything I needed to do it, what would I do?* There is freedom in these questions because they strip away the extraneous distractions that serve no purpose but to discourage or defeat you.

Passion Possibilities

As you move forward to unearth your passion, please know that you're not entering into a guessing game. Your passion is not going to be vague, nor will it be fleeting. It will be specific, and it will be something that sticks with you. That's not to say you may not have more than one passion in your lifetime. It's okay for your passion to shift throughout the course of your life because God is never through shaping us. But for now, concentrate on pinpointing your present passion. It will generally fall into one of three categories: people, roles/functions, or causes. [1]

Perhaps you are struggling not with doubting that you have any particular passion at all, but that you have too many! Maybe you look around at the world and get excited about any number of issues, subjects, and areas. That's good! But it can be overwhelming. You may feel just as stuck as the woman who feels that nothing at all interests her. In either case, these three general categories can help you either narrow the possibilities or stir your heart and prompt new possibilities.

People

The first category your passion may fall into is that of people. Perhaps your heart burns for a particular people group. Maybe it's children. Singles. Teenagers or youth. Women. South American or Chinese people. Seniors. Those who are grieving. Immigrants. Poor. Those with disabilities. The list could go on and on. This isn't a question of introversion or extroversion, it's a matter of heart. If you have a people passion, you long to be identified as someone who makes a difference in people's lives, regardless of whether you are an introvert or extrovert.

Paul made his people passion clear in Romans 15:20: "It has always been my ambition to preach the gospel where Christ was not known, so that I would not be building on someone else's foundation." Paul was burdened to declare the truth of Jesus Christ to those who did not know Him. It didn't matter where they lived, what they looked like, or how old they were. If they were lost without Christ, they mattered to Paul.

I have been given a passion for women. Not women of a particular country or region, not women of a certain age or socioeconomic status, but for women in general. This book is a product of my passion. I long to equip you with the truth and tools that will allow you as a woman to accept your true identity and move forward in the life that God has called you to. It's not that I want to make you have my same desire to reach and equip women. If we all cared about the same things, the many needs of the world would go unmet. So God draws our hearts to certain kinds of involvement for His purposes. And what fires me up is equipping you to be all God has made you to be!

Roles/Functions

There's simply no right or wrong passion when it is from the Lord. No passion is greater or less than another. If a certain people group does not pique your interest, perhaps your passion falls into the second category, that of a role or function—a thing that you love to do. Do you love learning and researching? Maybe you long to write. Disciple or mentor others. Teach. Speak. Create a beautiful environment. Fix things. Solve problems or develop systems. The list of various roles and functions is diverse and is an expression of our creative Creator.

One role might flat-out disinterest you, while another supercharges you with energy. People who develop systems fascinate me. That is a passion and gifting that couldn't be further from who I am. Thinking about it makes me want to yawn and curl up for a nap. But I love that some people are passionate about developing systems because their work is so beneficial in helping others (like me!) function more effectively.

Philip was passionate about teaching. Acts 8:29–31 says, "The Spirit told Philip, 'Go to that chariot and stay near it.' Then Philip ran up to the chariot and heard the man reading Isaiah the prophet. 'Do you understand what you are reading?' Philip asked. 'How can I,' he said, 'unless someone explains it to me?' So he invited Philip to come up and sit with him." Philip then explained the Scripture and told the man the Good News of Jesus Christ. They even stopped along their journey so Philip could baptize him. The man continued on his way rejoicing, and Philip went on his way preaching the Gospel in the surrounding area. Philip was passionate about the role of spreading the Gospel. It didn't matter where he was or who he was speaking to; he was in his element as a teacher and an evangelist.

Causes

The third category that your passion may fall into is that of a cause. Maybe you long to end discrimination or abortion. Perhaps you want to preserve the family or alleviate world hunger. Maybe pollution and recycling is your thing. Animal rights or health care. Election reform. First Amendment rights. Just look at a voter's pamphlet at election time to see a range of political causes alone that spark opinions and passions of every kind. Some politicians and activists give their entire lives to a cause.

Nehemiah was an activist. When he discovered that the wall of Jerusalem had been broken down and its gates burned with fire, he sat down and wept. He even mourned and fasted and prayed for several days (Neh. 1:3–4). Talk about a burden that caused him much distress! In the second chapter we discover that God had put it in his heart to do something for Jerusalem (Neh. 2:12). He was to create a plan and implement the rebuilding of Jerusalem's walls. This would not light my fire, but it did Nehemiah's because God placed it on his heart. The cause was one that filled the people with encouragement and hope for their future.

Of course not everything under the sun will energize your spirit and cause your heart to beat faster. Considering these three categories (people, roles/functions, and causes) will help guide your thinking and focus your passion possibilities. If you remain unclear about how, where, or in what way you are best suited to serve in your area of passion, consider the following two charts.[2]

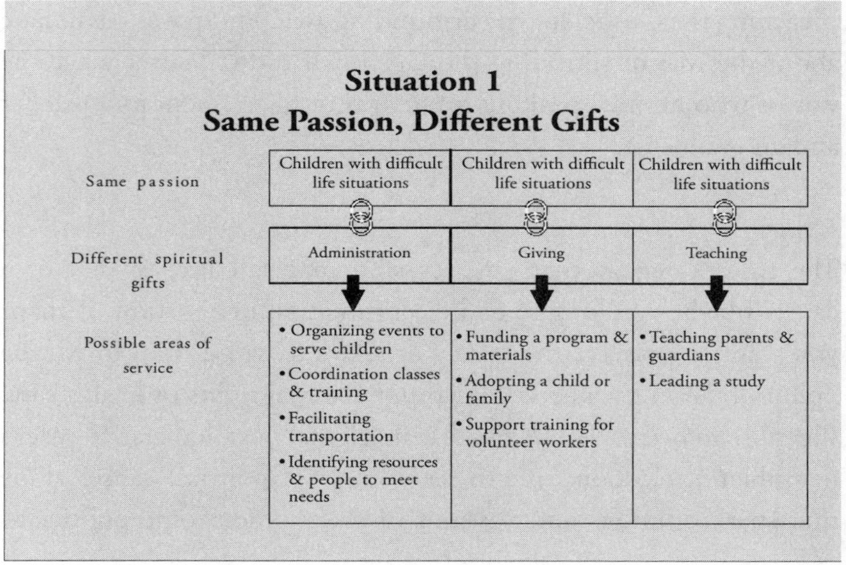

Situation 1
Same Passion, Different Gifts

Same passion	Children with difficult life situations	Children with difficult life situations	Children with difficult life situations
Different spiritual gifts	Administration	Giving	Teaching
Possible areas of service	• Organizing events to serve children • Coordination classes & training • Facilitating transportation • Identifying resources & people to meet needs	• Funding a program & materials • Adopting a child or family • Support training for volunteer workers	• Teaching parents & guardians • Leading a study

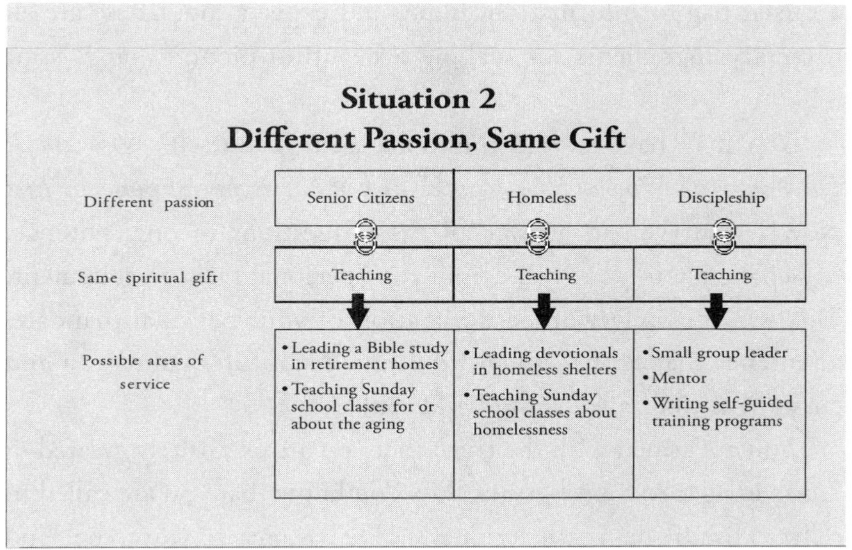

Situation 1 depicts what it might look like for three different people to have the same passion, but each with a different spiritual gift. Situation 2 shows three different people all with the same spiritual gift, but with different areas of passion. I hope this helps you see the possibilities that abound when it comes to determining how you might end up living out your passion based on who God has made you to be.

Your Personal Mission Statement

Take a moment to reflect on everything we've covered in this book. We have looked at what it means for you to be created uniquely female. We've thoroughly examined your true identity and inherent value as granted through the Trinity. I have pinpointed obstacles you will likely face on your journey to embracing the truth, and I've outlined tools for overcoming them. We've looked at the many facets that make you uniquely you. And now you've got yourself a mixed bag of information, hope, and expectation. These are all necessary ingredients for making a beautiful picture that is your life.

You may have started this book asking yourself, *Who am I? Do I matter? Why did God make me? What is my purpose in life?* Now I want you to answer all those questions in one sentence. My challenge to you is to define your personal mission statement. This is a concisely worded declaration of your personal mandate, a sentence that expresses why you exist. It captures your heart and passion, as well as your mind and soul.

You are armed with the truth that you are exquisitely created in God's image. You have great value. You know that you are called to reflect Him by being the unique *you* He has created you to be. And you know the essence of your purpose is to love and serve Him and others for His glory. Your mission statement focuses these concepts specifically to you. It is tailored to fit you, taking into account the intricacies of your God-given design.

I took a long, long time to discover my life's mission because I was a little rebellious and a lot fearful. Rebellion clouded my mind. I resisted being who God made me to be, thinking I knew better than He did how to live my life. And my fear of failure kept me from living out my personal mandate, which expresses my personal mission, because I let it freeze me in one place. I couldn't move forward. My adventurous husband likes to say, "If you're not living on the edge, you're taking up too much room." That cracks me up, but it strikes a chord, too. I've never tended toward living on the edge. Too risky! It was only after I submitted to my Creator in every way (which felt to me like jumping *off* the edge) that the foggy picture began to clear up and my heart began to thaw. I've come to realize that God really does have my best interests in mind.

He knows me better than I know myself, and He has never once abandoned or forsaken me.

Your mission statement is your bridge from here (your current life) to there (God's abundant life for you).

Discovering your life's mission might feel to you, too, like jumping off an edge you have always avoided. It might terrify you. I dare you to do it anyway. The view from where you land will be breathtaking. With clarity and purpose before you and passion burning within you, you will be motivated to liberally love and serve God and others. I guarantee there is no better way to spend your days. Living in the center of God's plan for your life is energizing. You overflow with His life and power. You are fundamentally motivated.

Your mission statement is your bridge from here (your current life) to there (God's abundant life for you). It is something that you will spend your lifetime fulfilling. You may have seasons when you go about fulfilling it in different ways. Those different approaches or activities are best defined along the lines of a vision statement. Vision statements are shorter-term strategies for accomplishing your long-term mission. They will change, often dramatically, in order to encompass three-, five-, or ten-year increments. Your lifetime mission statement, on the other hand, may change in small ways, but it will remain timeless in essence.

You may be tempted to ignore my challenge. You may not see the need for it. But consider that even Jesus Christ knew and declared His mission statement. In Luke 19:10 he states, "For the

Son of Man came to seek and save those who are lost" (NLT). That's it—clear, concise, to the point. Because Christ knew His mission, each and every day that He lived had purpose. And He changed the entire past, present, and future of humanity as a result.

Jesus knew where He was going. He lived out (and actually defined *for* us) all of the principles in this book. His identity came from His intimacy with the Father. His mission came out of His identity in relation to the Father. And He fulfilled the Father's will for His life by beginning with the end in mind. In the end, Christ died and rose in order to give life to you and me.

When you die to yourself—to your own self-abuse or to your self-oriented plans—it will not at all be the death of you. It will breed your new life. Consider Christ's words, "I tell you the truth, unless a kernel of wheat falls to the ground and dies, it remains only a single seed. But *if it dies, it produces many seeds*. The man who loves his life will lose it, while the man who hates his life in this world will keep it for eternal life. *Whoever serves me must follow me;* and where I am, my servant also will be. My Father will honor the one who serves me" (John 12:24–26, emphasis mine).

If you are willing to relinquish a skewed perspective so that you can embrace God's right perspective, blessing awaits you. He knows who you are. If you are willing to give up your life and your plans and your will in order that you may have God's life and God's plans and God's will for you, abundance will embrace you. This is what it is to forsake pride and embrace humility. A humble heart draws you closer to the heart of God, and there you can hear His gentle whisper.

Coming up with your mission statement will take time. It is a process that requires prayer, reflection, growing self-awareness, hoping, dreaming, and risking … not to mention several drafts.

You don't have to nail your mission statement right away. It will morph and take shape over time.

Ask God to give you clarity about who He has made you to be, and ask Him to reveal His vision for you. Be receptive to the Holy Spirit's prompting. He created you, so He has the answer you seek! Prayer is an exercise of trust. Just be prepared to accept the truth He will reveal about you … no matter how beautiful it may be!

As you receive clarity about your life's mission, be sure to write it down. God emphasizes the written word; He treasures it above many things. He knows we humans tend to forget. We constantly need to be reminded what is right and important. Consider that the Ten Commandments were written in stone and that in Habakkuk 2:2 He says, "Write my answer plainly on tablets, so that a runner can carry the correct message to others" (NLT). God could have shouted His message from heaven, but instead He wanted a human to write it down.

To commit your mission statement to paper is to value it. Experts say there is an 80 percent probability that you will achieve a goal if you're willing to put it in writing. And when you put it where you can see it every day, it will help you stay centered and focused, ready to maximize the gift of each day.

If you dread facing the blank page, face a "hidden" blank page. Don't show it to anyone! It's okay to not have it perfect. A first draft is a starting point. From there you can fine-tune it. Jesus' mission statement was succinct (Luke 19:10), and for the sake of clarity you will want your final statement to be brief. But let yourself start out with wild, run-on sentences if you have to! It took me many tries over several years to refine my own statement. As I learned more about myself and what God was teaching me, I would go back and alter it.

By the time you polish your mission statement and are truly pleased with it, you may want to share it with others. Sharing it with someone who knows you well can validate and reinforce the truth of your statement. Just remember as you are crafting it that you are doing this for an audience of One. It's not for anyone but God. He is the One you want to honor through your life's mission.

While your statement will answer why you are here, I would be misleading you if I implied that you will one day completely fulfill it. You are not Jesus. The author and perfecter of your faith has finished His work (Heb. 12:2), and it is done. But you are a work in progress, whether you are fourteen, forty-four, or eighty-four. God is not through with you yet (Phil. 1:6). He will continue shaping you. And as He does, He will never change your identity as His beloved, significant, and empowered image-bearing child.

I recently returned from a trip to Romania where I was privileged to teach a group of women, ages twenty to sixty, the key principles in this book. Romania is a former communist country that has a history of devaluing and abusing its women. One woman sat in the front row, often weeping, the entire weekend. She said that she had been abused by her husband their entire married life until he died, and that this was the first time she heard that anyone loved her.

Other women had tears in their eyes as well as they heard the truth about their value as God's image-bearing daughters. They were thrilled to hear that God the Father loves them unconditionally, that Jesus the Son elevated the status of women and gave them a significance that they could hardly believe, and that the Holy Spirit empowers them with competence. Without exception, they were deeply touched by this message of hope. I received a note at the end of the conference that expressed well what they felt: "This is the best, most precious time of my life. We learned first to look at the cross, and then to fly. Thank you."

Now it is *your* time to fly. Are you ready to live freely, abundantly, and confidently in God's perfect loving care? Say yes! And may the words of Christ comfort, strengthen, and encourage you every step of the way: "Peace be with you. As the Father has sent me, so I am sending you" (John 20:21, NLT).

Prayer

In closing, rather than praying to God, I encourage you instead to listen to Him. Meditate on these words. Don't fight them. Accept them. Imagine God Himself sitting across from you, holding your hands, and looking directly into your eyes:

> *"You are my beloved child. I chose you before the foundation of the world, to walk with Me along paths designed uniquely for you. Concentrate on keeping in step with Me, instead of trying to anticipate My plans for you. If you trust that My plans are to prosper you and not to harm you, you can relax and enjoy the present moment. Your hope and your future are rooted in heaven where eternal ecstasy awaits you. Nothing can rob you of your inheritance of unimaginable riches and well-being. Sometimes I grant you glimpses of your glorious future, to encourage you and spur you on. But your main focus should be staying close to Me. I set the pace in keeping with your needs and My purposes."*[3]

Questions for Reflection

This book will merely collect dust on your shelf and become a distant memory … unless you dare to do the difficult. If you want more than "head knowledge" as a result of reading this book, you must be willing to apply the truth to your own life. You must be willing to examine yourself and take tangible steps toward health, healing, and wholeness. If, when asked, "Who do you think you are?" you want to answer in both word and lifestyle, "I am a precious woman of God," you must take action now.

The Questions for Reflection will help you get started. I encourage you to set aside time to prayerfully and carefully answer each question. Use a separate journal where you feel free to write your innermost, honest answers and reflections. Let the questions prompt your prayers. No one will read your responses unless you choose to share them, so ask God to give you courage to answer each question from your heart of hearts, as you truly believe.

I further encourage you to go beyond journaling, praying, and completing the Questions for Reflection. My prayer for you is that you find a mentor, friend, or small group of women with whom to be in discussion about your God-given value. As well intentioned as we may be, and as sincerely as we want to make changes on our own, true life-change *usually* takes accountability. Our faulty beliefs, habits, and patterns of interacting with the world are so much a part of who we are. To change them, we need support, encouragement, and guidance from another godly woman or group of women. In humbly asking for help and practicing vulnerability, we open wide the door for God to move. And when He moves, He moves! The truth will move from a nice-sounding idea about your infinite worth to a powerful, transforming reality in your life.

Take a moment now to pray about how God would have you proceed. If the following prayer helps you get started, please do make it your own:

> *"God, I am sorry for undermining the infinite value You have so graciously given me. I have let doubt, fear, and my own experiences separate me from You, rather than letting Your truth heal me. Help me embrace my infinite value. I don't know how to get from here to there, Lord, and I need You to show me the way. Help me be honest with myself and with You as I go through this book and the Questions for Reflection. Show me if you would have me connect with a mentor, friend, or group of women to help me through. Keep me moldable and make me new. Amen."*

Questions for Reflection: Chapter 1

Our beliefs about ourselves, whether good or bad, impact how we live. When we believe the lie that we lack value, our negative thinking will lead us to rob the world and God of the unique contribution we were each created to make.

Use a separate sheet of paper or your journal to record the answers to these questions and any other thoughts you have.

1. Draw a line to represent the chronology of your life, from birth to present. We'll call this your "lifeline." Mark on it the dates or rough time periods that were significant in forming who you are today. Think about key achievements and decisions you made, significant people in your life, and noteworthy events. You can draw a jagged line with the beginning point being your birth and flags to represent later events. Another way to draw it is starting with a small circle representing your birth. Add a series of concentric circles moving outward—like tree rings—for the milestones of your life. Include events both happy and sad, key achievements, people who influenced or impacted you, and significant lessons learned.

   Consider including physical moves, friends, family, schools, jobs, deaths, and medical issues—major things that have significantly impacted your life. Don't worry about drawing it to scale or writing down everything that happened as a result of the event. Just take time to reflect on the major points in your life. This exercise will serve as a reference point as you respond to the questions throughout the Questions for Reflection. Below is an example of a young girl's lifeline.

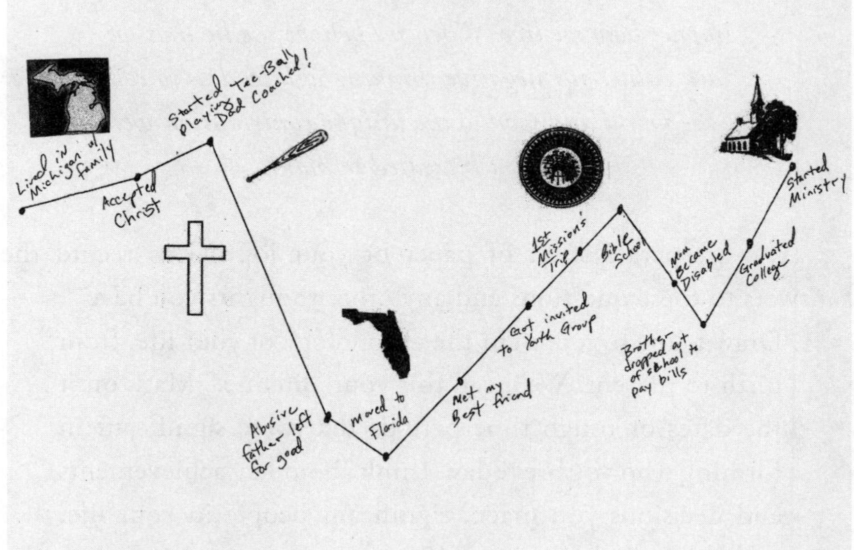

2. When you hear the phrase "your value as a woman," what do you think of?
3. What does being a woman mean to you?
4. Has your understanding of what it means to be a woman changed over the years? How?
5. What do you believe about your value?

Circle those that apply:

- I am "less than." Men are better.
- My failures and mistakes in life have made me "defective goods."
- What I do as a wife / mother / career woman is what defines me.
- Sexy, young, and beautiful women are valuable. I am not these.

- I must be perfect, or overachieve, to obtain value.
- I am valuable because I engage in ministry.
- My value lies in fulfilling my God-given roles.
- I am a child of God, precious in His sight.
- List any others that come to mind.

6. Where, and by whom, have you been taught about your value?
   - *Consider your childhood home.* What did you learn there? How did your father relate to you as a female while you were growing up? How did your father relate to your mother? If you did not have a father, how do you think the lack of a father figure shaped you? How did your siblings treat you?
   - *Consider your school.* What did you learn from your peers and teachers? How did your teachers relate to you? Do you remember any teacher in particular? What do you remember about them? How did the boys in the classroom relate to you? (For example, did they respect you? Or did they tend to make fun of your looks, your sensitivity, or the fact that you were different from them?)
   - *Consider your church.* What did you learn there? Did your church truly live by, or merely give lip service to, Galatians 3:28: "There is neither Jew nor Greek, slave nor free, male nor female, for you are all one in Christ Jesus."

> My dad did not know how to relate to me. He often squashed my enthusiasm. I interpreted his discomfort to mean there was something wrong with me, that I was flawed somehow. And as the fourth of four children, I wasn't given a voice (unless I talked really loud!) because the youngest was assumed to not know much. I interpreted this to mean I didn't know much and didn't have much value.

- *Consider the media.* What do you learn from the images and messages sent out thousands of times a day? What do movies, television, magazines, advertising, and others tell women about who we are?
- *What other influences* have shaped your beliefs about your value?

7. What is your purpose for reading this book? In what ways do you want to be changed?

Questions for Reflection: Chapter 2

Assumptions form our beliefs and thereby affect how we live. Often, our assumptions are rooted in faulty thinking, forming a disconnect, or gap, between the Christian worldview that we profess and the actual worldview we are living out. Excavating and correcting these assumptions will take deliberate and intentional focus.

1. Where do assumptions come from? (Six common sources were discussed in this chapter.)
2. List three or more assumptions you have made about yourself during significant time periods of your life. (Refer to the lifeline you made in the Questions for Reflection for chapter 1.) Which of these do you still believe?
3. Consider how your assumptions affect the way you live. First, think about your external behavior, including how you treat people, your habits and patterns, the decisions you make, and other behaviors. Make two columns. In the left-hand column, list the action or external behavior. In the right-hand column, list the assumption that motivates each behavior.
4. Refer to question 1. Which of the six originations of assumptions do you think have most shaped your own assumptions?
5. If you want to study in further depth the inerrancy of the Bible, pick a book or two listed in appendix 3, "Recommended Reading." List the titles and set a goal for when you want to complete them.

6. What is the first of the four steps for excavating your false assumptions (pp. 39–40)? Choose one or more of the four Gospels you would like to read with an eye for the stories involving women, and do it! (I would suggest Luke or John.) Also consider the following verses, and measure your assumptions next to them (i.e., ask how accurate your assumptions are): John 17:22–23; Galatians 3:28; Romans 5:8; 8:1, 38–39; Matthew 10:31; 2 Timothy 1:9; 1 John 3:1; 4:10; Ps. 118:6–7.
7. The second step for excavating your false assumptions (pp. 40–41) is seeking other perspectives. Do you want to do this? Why or why not? If you would like to, list the person or people you trust and with whom you would like to begin having deeper discussions.
8. The third step for excavating your false assumptions is choosing to develop a teachable spirit in a lifelong quest for learning (p. 41). Do you want this? If not, what within you fights this concept? (What are your obstacles?) If so, what excites you about this concept?

"We demolish arguments and every pretension that sets itself up against the knowledge of God, and we take captive every thought to make it obedient to Christ."
—2 Corinthians 10:5

"Therefore, if anyone is in Christ, he is a new creation; the old has gone, the new has come!"—2 Corinthians 5:17

"One thing I do: Forgetting what is behind and straining toward what is ahead, I press on toward the goal to win the prize for which God has called me heavenward in Christ Jesus."
—Philippians 3:13–14

"It is for freedom that Christ has set us free. Stand firm, then, and do not let yourselves be burdened again by a yoke of slavery."
—Galatians 5:1

9. The fourth and final step in excavating your false assumptions involves making a commitment to persevering, even when you want to give up and default to your old (and false!) assumptions and beliefs (p. 41). What will help you persevere? If you need accountability (and you probably do), consider writing down your goal and asking a trusted friend to be your partner in this journey. Consider writing down and saying aloud (daily, hourly, however often you need!) the verses in the sidebar.

> ❦ "Whatever is true, whatever is noble, whatever is right, whatever is pure, whatever is lovely, whatever is admirable—if anything is excellent or praiseworthy—think about such things."
>
> —Philippians 4:8
>
> ❦ "Do not conform any longer to the pattern of this world, but be transformed by the renewing of your mind."—Romans 12:2

Questions for Reflection: Chapter 3

The distorted view of woman has spread its roots since the fall of the first man and woman. The faulty assumptions you hold about yourself have been influenced by what has been passed down through the generations by philosophical thought, cultures, and religions around the world. These faulty assumptions are not biblical and do not represent a biblical worldview of a woman's identity.

> Note your thoughts and feelings in response to the first question. Then, if you find yourself bothered that it was Eve who first partook of the fruit, read Romans 5:12–21. Interestingly, it is Adam who is noted in the New Testament for the fall of mankind (Rom. 5:14).

1. When you consider Eve's role in the biblical account of the fall of man (Gen. 3), what do you think? What do you feel? Do you feel "less than" because Eve listened first to Satan? Why?
2. What is most shocking to you about what you have read in this chapter? What viewpoints expressed by the philosophers in this chapter do you witness or experience in the culture in which you live today? List the philosopher, the statement, and an example of where you have seen or experienced that perspective.
3. What negative viewpoints about women have you lived with? How have you dealt with what you were wrongly told about who you are?
4. What strikes you about Um Sarah's story? How do you relate to any of the specific things she says?

5. What has been your experience as a woman in the church? If you have been in more than one church, have you observed any differences with regard to the treatment of women? What were they?
6. On page 58 the author states, "The distorted and corrupt picture of woman does not reflect you. It does not define you. It is not your true identity." Ask yourself whether this is true or not in your life.

Questions for Reflection: Chapter 4

You, woman, have been created with love by God the Father. You are created in His image. Your intrinsic value is rooted in the fact that you are patterned after God, your heavenly Father.

1. Read and meditate on Psalm 139. Journal your response.
2. When you think of being created in God's image, what do you think about? How do you feel about this truth?
3. Of the ways listed in this chapter that you are created *like* God, focus on one and how you experience this likeness to God. Journal about or discuss what it reveals to you about His character.
4. Of the ways listed in this chapter that you are created *unlike* God, focus on one and journal about or discuss why you are thankful for this difference.
5. What in your life do you think has most shaped your definition of love? How does it compare with the reality of God's *hesed* love?
6. What objections do you have to the truth that your core need for love has already been met in the fact that you are created by God? On the other hand, how is this good news for you?
7. What in your life may be holding you back from experiencing God's love?

> "Through my first romantic relationship before I accepted Christ … I learned that human love can give a person value and dignity, but it can also be quite selfish. Later [after accepting Christ], I realized the only perfect love can only come from Jesus Christ, who sacrificed Himself on the cross. He has done so because we have great value in His eyes."
>
> —**Frances Ren,** one of my seminary students

> "When I read Genesis 1:31, 'God saw all that he had made, and it was very good,' I felt so touched by the Holy Spirit. All these years I had been laboring to be 'good' to prove my value. But God proclaims that He created me, and because of that fact I am good enough! This is such a liberating truth, relieving me from performance-based habitual behaviors."
>
> **—Frances Ren**

8. What would help you experience more fully God's love?
9. Use as many words as you can come up with to describe your earthly father, as you saw him, during your childhood years. If you did not have a father, do this exercise thinking about your primary care provider.
10. In your answer to question 9, circle the words that you have transferred onto God the Father, whether or not they reflect His true character. Of the false or wrong beliefs you have about your heavenly Father, which do you anticipate being the most difficult for you to change? Confess this to the Father, and ask Him to reveal His true self to you every day.
11. Read John 4:1–42. Remember that God made Himself visible as Jesus. Journal about or discuss your response.

Questions for Reflection: Chapter 5

You, woman, are God's female image bearer. Your femaleness has great value. It distinguishes you from man in a variety of ways, and is at the essence of your identity. Embracing these differences from your male counterparts frees you to move fully into your unique, God-given calling.

1. When you envision God, if you have tended to focus on His male characteristics and qualities to the exclusion of recognizing His female characteristics and qualities, how can you change your perspective to begin seeing Him in all His fullness?
2. What does the term *ezer kenegdo* mean? How does this term impact your current perception of yourself?
3. How do you see yourself being more relationally oriented than your male counterparts? Have you approached your relationships with men under the assumption that they are wired the same way you are? How?
4. What is your reaction to the scientific evidence that female and male brains are different? How does this influence your perception of men? Of yourself?
5. Think of a recent miscommunication you experienced with a man. Can it be attributed to any of the three ways listed in this chapter that we communicate differently?
6. Does the explanation of hierarchical and flat communication structures make sense to you? List the different areas of your life (home, work, various community involvements, etc.) and the type of communication structure you think is

best suited to each. Do you need to change your approach in any of these contexts?

7. God has made you uniquely female for a unique purpose. What are some other characteristics, behaviors, or communication patterns that distinguish you from men, and how can you move toward accepting and appreciating the differences?

Questions for Reflection: Chapter 6

You, woman, are significant. Jesus Christ, the second Person of the Trinity, lived to prove this every day He walked this earth. He broke the burden that women have been bearing since Eve. While people look at the exterior, He looks at your heart. While the world may shame you for being a woman, He elevates you. While people love conditionally, He loves you unconditionally.

1. How have you tried to satisfy your need to feel significant? Consider who you have you looked to in order to make you feel special, the activities have you pursued, the roles you have valued, etc.
2. Describe the kind of woman in your culture who would be today's equivalent of the Samaritan woman at the well. How do people treat her? What have you learned from Christ's actions in John 4:1–30 about how you could treat her?
3. Have you ever felt like the woman in John 8:1–11? Have you confessed your sin to Christ, or have you been avoiding Him? Would you like to approach Him now? (You know already He will respond lovingly, so you may draw near to Him without fear.)
4. Which of Christ's encounters with women recorded in the book of Luke strikes you most profoundly? (List as many as you like.) Why, and in what ways?
5. Have you ever felt like the woman in Mark 5:21–34? In what ways? How does Jesus' response to her strike you?

6. Christ empowers women to participate in His Kingdom work and share His Good News. How does that make you feel? In what ways can you respond within your sphere of influence?
7. Romans 8:1 says, "There is now no condemnation for those who are in Christ Jesus." What lesson from this chapter best proves this truth to you?
8. Galatians 3:28 says, "There is neither Jew nor Greek, slave nor free, male nor female, for you are all one in Christ Jesus." In the era of the apostle Paul (the author of this verse), this was a new paradigm of a woman's value. She was equal with man at the cross. How was Paul influenced by the teachings of Christ?
9. List some characteristics about Jesus Christ that you are thankful for. Talk to Him in prayer and ask Him to reveal more of Himself to you in your everyday life.

Questions for Reflection: Chapter 7

You are a competent, uniquely gifted woman of God. The Holy Spirit empowers you to live fruitfully and to bless the Body of Christ in a specific way through spiritual gifts.

> "And hope does not disappoint us, because God has poured out his love into our hearts by the Holy Spirit, whom he has given us."—Romans 5:5

1. Define *competence.* What is a practical example of a task you feel competent to do?
2. Now recognizing your need for competence as a critical component to accepting who God made you to be, on a scale of 1–10, how much more competent as a valuable woman of God would you like to feel?
3. What do you think and feel when you hear that the Holy Spirit chooses to be with you all of the time, everywhere?
4. What does it mean to be empowered? What do you think and feel as you realize you don't have to rely upon your own resources, but that you are in fact empowered by the Holy Spirit to live the life God has called you to?
5. In what ways are all believers empowered by the Holy Spirit?
6. What is the one grand reason God created you (and all people)?
7. What is the definition of a spiritual gift?
8. What sets spiritual gifts apart from natural talents or fruit of the Spirit?

> For further study on spiritual gifts, examine these five key sections of Scripture: Romans 12; 1 Corinthians 12 and 14; Ephesians 4; 1 Peter 4.

9. Review the lifeline you completed after chapter 1 to help you reflect on those things you know or have been told you have been good at, have done well, or have enjoyed doing. List them. If you have completed a spiritual gifts assessment, mark which ones are spiritual gifts. (See appendix 2, "Spiritual Gifts and Definitions.") Then list what you consider to be your natural talents. If you're not sure what you are naturally talented or spiritually gifted to do, see appendix 3, "Recommended Reading." Choose a resource and write it down. Set a goal for the date you want to complete it.

Questions for Reflection: Chapter 8

Learning to see yourself as God sees you is a lifelong process. It requires taking intentional action steps. In so doing, you will experience great freedom in being yourself; you will bring glory to God while experiencing personal fulfillment!

1. What do you think when I say that embracing your true identity and value is a lifelong journey? Describe any trepidation you may have.
2. If you want to move forward, what are the four specific "chair legs" you need to commit to every day? Write each on a three-by-five index card. On the back of each, write key thoughts from this book or verses in the Bible that will help you accomplish them. Keep the cards where you will see them every day (perhaps taped to your bathroom mirror, on the refrigerator, or in your purse).
3. Read what the Bible says about who you are in appendix 1. Pick three (or more) of those verses to commit to memory this week. Also memorize the corresponding "I am" statement and the "address" (the biblical reference, e.g., John 15:15).
4. What are the four main obstacles that threaten to keep you from accepting and internalizing your true identity? Pick one to focus on, and list which specific problems you currently face that it encompasses.
5. List the six steps it takes to remove an obstacle or roadblock. Choose an obstacle you named in question 4 and apply the six "roadblock removal" steps to it: write

out what each step means to you, and how you might apply it to your issue. That may mean noting various Bible verses, taking time with God in prayer, seeking counsel or accountability from a friend, and writing an "I will" statement. (Don't settle for "I would like to … " Instead, write, "I will … " and ask God to help you accomplish it.) See sample journal entry at the end of the questions for this chapter.

6. This chapter emphasizes your ability to *choose*. Do you agree or disagree that you have the freedom to choose the road you will take? Do you *feel* that you have no choice? Why? What does God's word say about choosing? (See Joshua 24:15; Proverbs 8:10; Proverbs 16:16; and Philippians 4:8–9, 13.)
7. In what ways was Paul a visionary Christian? Would you like to be one? If so, write an "I will" sentence about that and commit to it.

Sample Journal Entry

Steps to removing my roadblock

Roadblock: *Mind clouded by sin*

1. Identify the problem: *Letting others' opinions control me*

2. Discover God's truth:

"The sinful mind is hostile to God. It does not submit to God's law, nor can it do so. Those controlled by the sinful nature cannot please God. You, however, are controlled not by the sinful nature but by the Spirit, if the Spirit of God lives in you."—Romans 8:7–9

"Am I now trying to win the approval of men, or of God? Or am I trying to please men? If I were still trying to please men, I would not be a servant of Christ."—Galatians 1:10

3. Confess my sin and receive God's grace:

(I did this through a much longer prayer, but what I wrote below got me started.)

Lord, I confess I have idolized others' opinions. I have let them mean more to me than what You think. I am sorry, and I ask Your forgiveness. I humbly seek You and thank You for forgiving me.

4. Exercise courage to embrace God's truth:

Others' opinions change all the time and are entirely subjective. I cannot keep altering my words and deeds based on what I think might earn me favor. So today I will live for an audience of One. I will respond to God, and live to honor and please Him alone. This week I will memorize Romans 8:7–9 and Galatians 1:10.

5. Cultivate humility:

I will humble myself by taking time every morning this week to recognize that I am nothing without Jesus Christ. If throughout the day I begin to alter my actions based on what I think someone will think of me, I will stop in my tracks and remember how Christ gave His life so that I might live free from these chains.

6. Choose to obey, walk in the truth, and renew my mind with the Word of God:

I have decided today to walk in the truth. The truth is:

"I have come that they may have life, and have it to the full."

—John 10:10

Constantly trying to please or impress others is not the abundant life Christ came to give me. I choose to no longer be bound by what I think they think. I will not worry this week about failing to meet others' unspoken expectations of me.

I decide today to RENEW MY MIND with God's Word:

"But we have the mind of Christ."—1 Corinthians 2:16

"Do not conform any longer to the pattern of this world, but be

transformed by the renewing of your mind."—Romans 12:2

These verses tell me that the key is what I think about. I have too long been thinking about what others think of me. And that is my problem—my focus is wrong. I want to instead focus on things pleasing to God.

7. Enjoy the process

I will remind myself that this is a daily process and it's not going to be easy all the time. But I want to begin living now the way that I want to live for all eternity—pleasing my Savior. I will "Rejoice in the Lord always. I will say it again: Rejoice!" (Phil. 4:4). The joy of the Lord is my strength (Neh. 8:10). His peace will guard my heart and my mind (Phil. 4:7).

Questions for Reflection: Chapter 9

Your personal mandate is the "glove" that fits
on the "hand" of your true identity as
God's precious image bearer.
It is the unique way you live out your mandate
to love God and serve others.

1. When you picture the "prism of humanity" with its countless facets of individuals, what do you think? How does this analogy help you see your part in the Body of Christ?
2. Have you confused roles and jobs with your identity? What do you feel when you read that the job someone holds is not their identity, and does not have to be their personal mandate?
3. Discovering your personal mandate involves making an accurate self-assessment. On a scale from 1 to 10, with 10 being perfectly, how well do you know yourself right now? What do you think you still need to learn?
4. Is there a role you have performed in the past (at a job, as a volunteer, or in another capacity) that did *not* fit you well? List one (or more). What did you dislike about it? What did you learn about yourself in the process?
5. Is there a role you have performed in the past (at a job, as a volunteer, or in another capacity) that *did* fit you well? List one (or more). What did you like about it? What did you learn about yourself in the process?
6. Would you like to know yourself better? How will you accomplish this? Write the name of someone you trust to

ask for honest feedback about your personality, strengths and weaknesses, gifts and talents, etc. Set up a time to meet and chat about this. List a resource or two that will help you perform a thorough self-inventory and make an accurate self-assessment. Commit to reading and completing it by a certain date.

7. How do you feel when you think about our mandate to love God and serve others? What does your answer say about what is motivating you?
8. What are the four life areas that you must nurture in order to grow, develop, and stay the course?
9. What is one area that most needs your attention? List the action steps you will take to develop this part of your life.

Questions for Reflection: Chapter 10

Discovering your God-given passion will allow you to serve Him and love others in a way that both invigorates and fulfills you. Writing your personal mission statement will punctuate your days with purpose as you confidently live out your unique identity all the days of your life.

1. How is passion defined in this chapter?
2. What is the difference between something that might get you out of bed in the morning and a God-given passion?
3. What traits mark a driven person who is without passion?
4. What are some of the obstacles that Satan has used to prevent you from abundant living? Arm yourself for battle by memorizing Ephesians 6:10–18.
5. If your fears, worries, and doubts are truly tissue-paper thin, how might you be living differently?
6. What are some cues or indicators that may help you discover your passion?
7. Look at your lifeline again (chapter 1). Think about a particular crucible or crisis that you have faced (or are perhaps now facing). What did it show you about what's important in life? Has it impacted what interests you, or how you want to invest your time?
8. What are the three categories of passion?
9. Have you defined your God-given passion? If so, write it down. If you're not sure what it is, brainstorm the possibilities considering the cues you listed for question

6, the three categories of passion, and the charts shown on pages 188–189.

10. What question does a personal mission statement answer?
11. If you can define your mission statement now, write it down. If you need a template to help you get started, use this one. Replace the bold words to customize it as your own:

    "I believe God has uniquely created me, His female image bearer, as someone who is designed with the **gifts of teaching and leading** (insert your spiritual gifts and natural talents) and a passion for **women** (insert your specific passion) so that I will **inspire, influence, and equip others to fulfill their own God-given calling** (insert ways you can serve God and love others).

(Keep in mind that *how* you accomplish your mission is best captured through a vision statement. You do not need capture the specific *how* in your mission statement.)

Gradually work on refining and simplifying your statement. **Sample**:

I am here to inspire and equip women to fulfill their unique, God-given calling in life.

Appendix 1

Who Am I?

Gen. 1:26	I am created in God's image.
Psa. 8:5	I am crowned with glory and honor.
Psa. 139:14	I am fearfully and wonderfully made.

As a believer in Christ:

Matt. 5:13	I am the salt of the earth.
Matt. 5:14	I am the light of the world.
John 15:1, 5	I am part of the true vine, a branch of Christ's life.
John 15:15	I am Christ's friend.
John 15:16	I am chosen and appointed by Christ to bear fruit that lasts.
Rom. 6:18	I am a slave of righteousness.
Rom. 6:22	I am enslaved to God.
Rom. 8:14–15	I am an adopted child of God and He is my heavenly Father. (NLT)
Rom. 8:16–17	I am an heir of God and co-heir with Christ.
1 Cor. 3:16	I am a temple of God. His Spirit lives in me.
1 Cor. 6:17	I am one in spirit with Him.
1 Cor. 12:27	I am a part of the Body of Christ.
2 Cor. 5:17	I am a new creation.
2 Cor. 5:18	I am reconciled to God.
2 Cor. 5:18	I am a minister of reconciliation.
Gal. 3:26	I am a son of God.

Gal. 3:28	I am one with Christ and all believers. I am equal.
Gal. 4:6–7	I am an heir of God since I am a son of God.
Eph. 1:1	I am a saint. (See also 1 Cor. 1:2 [NASB]; Phil. 1:1; Col. 1:2 [NASB].)
Eph. 2:4–5	I am alive with Christ.
Eph. 2:8	I am saved by grace.
Eph. 2:10	I am God's workmanship created (born anew) in Christ Jesus to do good work that He planned beforehand for me to do.
Eph. 2:19	I am a fellow citizen with the rest of God's people.
Eph. 2:19	I am a member of God's family. (NLT)
Eph. 4:22–24	I am righteous and holy.
Phil. 3:20	I am a citizen of heaven and seated in heaven right now. (See Eph. 2:6.)
Col. 2:10	I am made complete in Him. (NASB)
Col. 3:1	I am raised up with Christ.
Col. 3:3	I am hidden with Christ in God.
Col. 3:12	I am chosen of God, holy, and dearly loved.
1 Thess. 1:4	I am chosen and loved by God.
Heb. 3:1	I am one who shares in the heavenly calling.
Heb. 3:14	I will share in Christ's life.
1 Pet. 2:5	I am one of God's living stones and am being built up (in Christ) as a spiritual house.
1 Pet. 2:9	I am one of a chosen people, a royal priesthood, a holy nation, the people of God.
1 Pet. 2:11	I am an alien and a stranger to this world.
1 Pet. 5:8	I am an enemy of the devil.

1 John 3:1–2	I am a child of God. I will be like Christ when He returns.
1 John 5:18	I am born of God and the evil one cannot touch me. (NLT)

Appendix 2

Spiritual Gifts and Definitions

Administration:

The Spirit-empowered ability to efficiently organize information, people, and things toward a common goal.

Apostleship:

The Spirit-empowered ability to pioneer and develop new churches and ministries.

Discernment:

The Spirit-empowered ability to distinguish between truth and error, between good and evil spirits, differentiating between good and evil.

Encouragement/Exhortation:

The Spirit-empowered ability to encourage, strengthen faith, comfort, instruct, or urge to action.

Evangelism:

The Spirit-empowered ability and passion to effectively communicate the Gospel to unbelievers with great effect.

Faith:

The Spirit-empowered ability to believe and act on God's promises with confidence in His ability to fulfill His purposes.

Giving:

The Spirit-empowered ability to determine physical needs

and share resources to further the work of the Lord, giving with cheerfulness and liberality.

Healing:

The Spirit-empowered ability to call upon God to heal the sick by any supernatural means.

Helps:

The Spirit-empowered ability to help persons complete God-given tasks by working alongside them.

Interpretation:

The Spirit-empowered ability to make known to the Body of Christ the message of one who is speaking in an unknown language.

Knowledge:

The Spirit-empowered ability to seek out, understand, and effectively organize a body of biblical information.

Leadership:

The Spirit-empowered ability to cast vision and oversee, direct, and motivate God's people to harmoniously accomplish the purposes of God.

Mercy:

The Spirit-empowered ability to perceive the hurts people are suffering and show Christ's compassion without judgment.

Miracles:

The Spirit-empowered ability to authenticate the ministry of

God through supernatural acts that glorify Him.

Prophecy:

The Spirit-empowered ability to recognize sin and speak forth God's truth with power in a manner relevant for understanding, correction, repentance, or edification.

Serving:

The Spirit-empowered ability to joyfully provide practical support in meeting the physical needs of others.

Shepherding (Pastor-Teacher):

The Spirit-empowered ability to nurture and care for the spiritual needs of people, using God's Word to guide them to spiritual maturity.

Teaching:

The Spirit-empowered ability to understand, clearly communicate, and apply the Word of God so that the listeners become spiritually mature.

Tongues:

The Spirit-empowered ability to speak, worship, or pray in a language unknown to the speaker.

Wisdom:

The Spirit-empowered ability to apply a spiritual truth effectively from God's Word to meet a specific need.

List of Spiritual Gifts found in New Testament

1 Corinthians 12	**Romans 12:6–11**	**Ephesians 4:11**
Wisdom		Apostle
	Encouragement	Evangelist
Knowledge	Giving	Prophet
	Mercy	Shepherd (Pastor-Teacher)
Faith	Prophesying	
	Teacher	
Healing	Service	
Miracles	Leadership	
Prophecy		
Discernment	**1 Corinthians 14:1–25** Speaking in different tongues	**1 Peter 4:10–11** Prophesy
Tongues	Prophecy	Serving
Interpretation	Interpretation	
Apostle		
Teacher		
Helps		
Administration		

The Gifts of the Spirit Divided into Groups

Speaking Gifts	Serving Gifts
Wisdom	Faith
Knowledge	Healing
Prophecy	Miraculous powers
Tongues	Service
Interpretation	Discernment
Apostle	Helps
Teacher	Administration
Encouragement	Giving
Leadership	Mercy
Evangelist	
Pastor-Teacher	

Appendix 3

Recommended Reading

For an understanding of how secular, non-Christian worldviews have impacted today's church and its view of women (chapter 1):

- *Total Truth: Liberating Christianity from Its Cultural Captivity* by Nancy Pearcey
- *Nurturing the Nations: Reclaiming the Dignity of Women in Building Healthy Cultures* by Darrow Miller with Stan Guthrie
- *Truth and Transformation: A Manifesto for Ailing Nations* by Vishal Mangalwadi

For further understanding related to wrong assumptions (chapter 2):

- *The Lies We Believe* by Chris Thurman
- *Telling Yourself the Truth* by William Backus and Marie Chapian
- *When Life and Beliefs Collide* by Carolyn Custis James

For an understanding about the Bible and its authority as God's revealed Truth (chapter 3):

- *A General Introduction to the Bible* by Norman L. Geisler and William E. Nix
- *Biblical Inspiration* by I. Howard Marshall
- *Inspiration and Canonicity of the Scriptures* by R. Laird Harris
- *Scripture and Truth* edited by D. A. Carson and John D. Woodbridge

- *The Authority of the Bible* by John R. W. Stott
- *Systematic Theology* by Wayne Grudem

For an understanding of culture in biblical times (chapter 3):

- *Josephus: The Essential Writings* translated and edited by Paul L. Meier
- *Unveiled* by Francine Rivers (historical fiction)
- *Women and the Genesis of Christianity* by Ben Witherington III
- *Man and Woman in Biblical Perspective* by James B. Hurley
- *The Gospel of Ruth* by Carolyn Custis James
- *The IVP Bible Background Commentary: New Testament* by Craig S. Keener

For further understanding of God as our Creator and ourselves as God's image bearers (chapter 4):

- *Created in God's Image* by Anthony A. Hoekema
- *The Knowledge of the Holy* by A. W. Tozer
- *Systematic Theology* by Wayne Grudem

For further study and understanding of the differences between men and women / male and female (chapter 5):

- *You Just Don't Understand: Women and Men in Conversation* by Deborah Tannen
- *For Women Only: What You Need to Know About the Inner Lives of Men* by Shaunti Feldhahn
- *Men and Women: Enjoying the Difference* by Larry Crabb
- *Laugh Your Way to a Better Marriage* by Mark Gungor

- *Men Are from Israel, Women Are from Moab* by Norm Wakefield and Jody Brolsma

For further study and life-application of your significance in Christ Jesus (chapter 6):

- *The Search for Significance: Seeing Your True Worth Through God's Eyes* by Robert S. McGee
- *The Call: Finding and Fulfilling the Central Purpose of Your Life* by Os Guinness
- *The Divine Conspiracy: Rediscovering Our Hidden Life In God* by Dallas Willard

For further study of the Holy Spirit and your spiritual gifts (chapter 7):

Online Resources:

- *BreakThru: A Spiritual Gifts Diagnostic Inventory* by Ralph Ennis available to order at http://www.leadconsulting-usa.com/.
- http://www.brucebugbee.com. Click on "Resources" or "Training."
- Saddleback Church: http://www.saddlebackresources.com/. Click on "Purpose Driven Life" to see additional resources.
- http://www.preceptaustin.org/spiritual_gifts_chart.htm

Free online assessments:

- http://www.shapediscovery.com/
- http://www.churchgrowth.org/analysis/intro.php
- "Spiritual Gifts Discovery Test" from Little Union Baptist Church, Bloomington, Indiana. Go to

www.littleunion.org; click on "Related Links" and on "Spiritual Gifts Discovery Test." Or download directly from www.littleunion.org/LUBC-Test.doc.

Books:

- *The Purpose Driven Life* by Rick Warren
- *Discover Your Spiritual Gifts the Network Way* by Bruce Bugbee
- *What You Do Best in the Body of Christ* by Bruce Bugbee
- *Keep in Step with the Spirit* by J. I. Packer

To get to know yourself better, on your way to discovering the right glove for your unique hand, your personal mandate (chapter 9):

Online resource:

- *BreakThru: A Primary Roles Diagnostic Inventory* by Ralph Ennis available to order at http://www.leadconsulting-usa.com/. Click on "Breakthru Series"

Free online assessment:

- The Primary Color Assessment by Rick Smith available at http://www.primarycolorsassessment.com/

Books:

- *Personality Plus: How to Understand Others by Understanding Yourself* by Florence Littauer
- *StrengthsFinder 2.0* by Tom Rath

- *Maximizing Your Effectiveness: How to Discover and Develop Your Divine Design* by Aubrey Malphurs
- *The Power of Uniqueness* by Arthur F. Miller Jr. with William Hendricks
- *Understanding How Others Misunderstand You* by Ken Voges and Ron Braund

To help you define, prioritize, and manage your life (chapter 9):

- *Margin* by Richard A. Swenson
- *Balancing Life's Demands* by J. Grant Howard
- *Ordering Your Private World* by Gordon MacDonald

To help you define your personal mission (chapter 10):

- *LifeWork: A Biblical Theology for What You Do Every Day* by Darrow L. Miller
- *Chazown: A Different Way to See Your Life* by Craig Groeschel
- *The Intentional Woman: A Guide to Experiencing the Power of Your Story* by Carol Travilla and Joan C. Webb
- *The Grand Weaver: How God Shapes Us Through the Events in Our Lives* by Ravi Zacharias
- *How to Find Your Mission in Life* by Richard Nelson Bolles
- *What You Do Best in the Body of Christ* by Bruce Bugbee

- *Make a Life, Not Just a Living* by Ron Jenson
- *Mindmapping: Your Personal Guide to Exploring Creativity and Problem-Solving* by Joyce Wycoff

Notes

Part One

1. McGerr, *Johnny Lingo.* [Story is partially based on this pamphlet.]

Chapter 1

1. Pearcey, *Total Truth,* 348.

Chapter 2

1. Larson, *Illustrations for Preaching,* 167.
2. Belenky and others, *Women's Ways of Knowing*, 5.
3. Covey, *7 Habits,* 29.

Chapter 3

1. Pantel and others, *A History of Women,* 51.
2. Durant, *The Story of Civilization,* vol. 1, *Our Oriental Heritage,* 35.
3. Bristow, *What Paul Really Said,* 4.
4. Women in the Bible, "The Woman with Prolonged Menstruation," http:/www.womeninthebible.net/2.6.Menstruating_woman.htm).
5. Pantel and others, *A History of Women,* 51.
6. Durant, *The Story of Civilization,* vol. 2, *The Life of Greece,* 51–52.
7. Demosthenes, *Against Neaera,* 122.
8. Durant, *The Story of Civilization,* vol. 3, *Caesar and Christ,* 56–57.
9. AlMunajjed, *Women in Saudi Arabia,* 12–13.
10. Parshall and Parshall, *Lifting the Veil*, 22.
11. Koran 4:34.

12. Parshall and Parshall, *Lifting the Veil*, 54.
13. *Sahih Bukhari,* vol. 4, bk. 54, "Beginning of Creation," no. 464.
14. *Sahih Bukhari,* vol. 7, bk. 62, "Wedlock, Marriage (Nikaah)," no. 30.
15. *Sahih Bukhari,* trans. M. Muhsin Khan, vol. 4, bk. 54, "Beginning of Creation," no. 460. An alternate translation would be, "Evil omen is in the women, the house and the horse."
16. Sirach 22:3, Revised Standard Version.
17. Witherington, *Women and the Genesis of Christianity,* 3.
18. Martos and Hégy, *Equal at the Creation,* 131.
19. Durant, *The Story of Civilization,* vol. 4, *The Age of Faith,* 825.
20. Ibid., 825.
21. Martos and Hégy, *Equal at the Creation,* 131–2.

Chapter 4

1. Crabb, *Understanding People,* chap. 6.
2. Hoekema, *Created in God's Image,* 16.
3. James, *The Gospel of Ruth,* 115.
4. Ibid., 117.
5. Tozer, *Knowledge of the Holy,* 1.

Chapter 5

1. Grudem, *Systematic Theology,* 439–40 .
2. David Eckman, "Gender Relationships," *Life Solutions Series on Relationships,* BWGI Ministries Web site. http://www.whatgodintended.com/content/relationship-gender.asp.
3. Alter, *Genesis,* 9.
4. Eldredge and Eldredge, *Captivating,* 32.
5. James, *The Gospel of Ruth,* 211.

6. Gilligan, *In a Different Voice,* 159–60.

7. Brizendine, *The Female Brain,* 12.

8. Ibid., 21.

9. Ibid., 4.

10. Ibid., 29.

11. Ibid., 4.

12. Ibid., 5.

13. Ibid., 5.

14. Saucy and TenElshof, *Women and Men,* 233.

15. Sethi, "The Truth about Boys and Girls," 44.

16. Tannen, *You Just Don't Understand,* 227–8.

17. Heim, *The Power Dead-Even Rule* and *Invisible Rules,* videos.

Chapter 6

1. Lightfoot, *Commentary on the New Testament*, ed. Robert Gandell, 3:275.

2. Witherington, *Women and the Genesis of Christianity,* 201.

3. Ibid., 204.

4. Ibid., 101.

5. Ibid., 102.

6. Ibid., 9.

7. Ibid., 9.

8. Sayers, *Are Women Human?* 68–69.

Chapter 7

1. Horton, ed., *The Portable Seminary,* 147.

2. *Dictionary.com*, s.v. "competence," http://dictionary.reference.com/browse/competence (accessed December 29, 2009).

3. Grudem, *Systematic Theology,* 634.

4. *Dictionary.com*, s.v. "empower," http://dictionary.reference.com/

browse/empower (accessed December 30, 2009).

Chapter 8

1. Guinness, *Time for Truth,* 110.

2. Mulholland, *Invitation to a Journey,* 19.

Chapter 9

1. Kierkegaard, *Purity of Heart,* 72.

2. Sweet, *AquaChurch,* 90.

Chapter 10

1. Bugbee, *What You Do Best,* 35–36.

2. Used by permission of Scottsdale Bible Church. Original source unknown.

3. Young, *Jesus Calling,* 177.

Bibliography

AlMunajjed. See Munajjed, Mona Al-.

Alter, Robert. Genesis: Translation and Commentary. New York: W. W. Norton, 1997.

Belenky, Mary Field, Jill Mattuck Tarule, Nancy Rule Goldberger, and Blythe McVicker Clinchy. *Women's Ways of Knowing.* 10th anniv. ed. New York: Basic Books, 1997.

Bristow, John T. *What Paul Really Said About Women.* New York: HarperCollins, 1988.

Brizendine, Louann. *The Female Brain.* New York: Broadway Books, 2006.

Bugbee, Bruce. *What You Do Best in the Body of Christ: Discover Your Spiritual Gifts, Personal Style, and God-Given Passion.* Grand Rapids, MI: Zondervan, 1995.

Covey, Stephen R. *The 7 Habits of Highly Effective People.* New York: Simon and Shuster, 1989.

Crabb, Larry. *Understanding People.* Grand Rapids, MI: Zondervan, 1987.

Durant, Will. *The Story of Civilization.* Vol. 1, *Our Oriental Heritage.* New York: Simon and Schuster, 1963.

Durant, Will. *The Story of Civilization.* Vol. 2, *The Life of Greece.* New York: Simon and Schuster, 1966.

Durant, Will. *The Story of Civilization.* Vol. 3, *Caesar and Christ.* New York: Simon and Schuster, 1972.

Durant, Will. *The Story of Civilization.* Vol. 4, *The Age of Faith.* New York: Simon and Schuster, 1950.

Eldredge, John, and Stasi Eldredge. *Captivating: Unveiling the Mystery of a Woman's Soul.* Nashville, TN: Nelson, 2005.

Gilligan, Carol. *In a Different Voice: Psychological Theory and*

Women's Development, 6th ed. Cambridge, MA: Harvard University Press, 1993.

Grudem, Wayne. *Systematic Theology: An Introduction to Biblical Doctrine.* Grand Rapids, MI: Zondervan, 1994.

Guinness, Os. *Time for Truth: Living Free in a World of Lies, Hype, and Spin.* Grand Rapids, MI: Baker Books, 2000.

Heim, Pat. *The Power Dead-Even Rule* and *Invisible Rules: Men, Women, and Teams.* Videos. San Jose, CA: Cynosure Productions, LTD and KTEH for CorVision. [I am indebted to Dr. Pat Heim's videos of her lectures for these insights.]

Hoekema, Anthony A. *Created in God's Image.* Grand Rapids, MI: William B. Eerdmans, 1986.

Horton, David, ed. *The Portable Seminary: A Master's Level Overview in One Volume.* Bloomington, MN: Bethany House, 2006.

James, Carolyn Custis. *The Gospel of Ruth: Loving God Enough to Break the Rules.* Grand Rapids, MI: Zondervan, 2008.

Kierkegaard, Søren. *Purity of Heart Is to Will One Thing.* Radford, VA: Wilder Publications, 2008.

Larson, Craig Brian, ed. *Illustrations for Preaching and Teaching: From "Leadership Journal."* Grand Rapids, MI: Baker Books, 1993.

Lightfoot, John. *A Commentary on the New Testament from the Talmud and Hebraica.* Edited by Robert Gandell. Oxford: Oxford University Press, 1859.

Martos, Joseph and Pierre Hégy, eds. *Equal at the Creation: Sexism, Society and Christian Thought.* Toronto: University of Toronto Press, 1998.

McGerr, Patricia. *Johnny Lingo and the Eight-Cow Wife.* Newport

Beach, CA: KenningHouse, 1982. [Pamphlet]

Mulholland, M. Robert, Jr. *Invitation to a Journey: A Road Map for Spiritual Formation.* Downers Grove, IL: InterVarsity Press, 1993.

Munajjed, Mona Al-. *Women in Saudi Arabia Today*. New York: St Martin's Press, 1997.

Pantel, Pauline Schmitt, ed. *A History of Women in the West.* Vol. 1, *From Ancient Goddesses to Christian Saints.* Series editors Georges Duby and Michelle Perrot. Translated by Arthur Goldhammer. Cambridge, MA: Harvard University Press, 1994.

Parshall, Phil, and Julie Parshall. *Lifting the Veil.* Waynesboro, GA: Gabriel Publishing, 2002.

Pearcey, Nancy. *Total Truth.* Wheaton, IL: Crossway, 2005.

Saucy, Robert L., and Judith K. TenElshof, eds. *Women and Men in Ministry: A Complementary Perspective.* Chicago: Moody Press, 2001.

Sayers, Dorothy. *Are Women Human?* Grand Rapids, MI: William B. Eerdmans, 1971.

Sethi, Anita. "The Truth about Boys and Girls." *Babytalk*, August 2008, 44.

Sweet, Leonard. *AquaChurch: Essential Leadership Arts for Piloting Your Church in Today's Fluid Culture.* Loveland, CO: Group Publishing, 1999.

Tannen, Deborah. *You Just Don't Understand: Women and Men in Conversation.* New York: Ballantine Books, 1990.

Tozer, A. W. *The Knowledge of the Holy.* New York: HarperCollins, 1961.

Witherington, Ben, III. *Women and the Genesis of Christianity.* Cambridge: Cambridge University Press, 1990.

Young, Sarah. *Jesus Calling.* Nashville, TN: Thomas Nelson, 2004.

About the Authors

Dr. Kristin Beasley, founder and executive director of Greater Reach Ministries, is an author, international speaker, and teacher with more than thirty years' ministry experience. She established Greater Reach in 2006 to assist women around the world in finding their life's meaning and purpose.

Formerly the dean of women at Phoenix Seminary for ten years, Kristin is now an adjunct faculty member, teaching courses in the women's studies program. In addition to developing this program, she also founded the seminary's Women with Vision conference and directed it for fourteen years. Her husband, Fred, is the pastor of world outreach at Scottsdale Bible Church, where Kristin has also served in women's ministry leadership.

Kristin's extensive knowledge and experience in the area of women's issues and concerns make her a sought-after speaker, thinker, and teacher. She has shared good news with women from Guatemala to Kenya, Russia to Romania. Her can-do enthusiasm for life fires her passion to encourage, equip, and empower women for life and ministry.

Kristin and Fred have been married thirty-seven years and have two grown sons. They make their home in Scottsdale, Arizona, and enjoy retreats to their cabin in Forest Lakes, Arizona.

Jodi Carlson is passionate about the Lord Jesus and His work in people's lives. Formerly an editor with *Brio* and *Brio & Beyond* magazines, her heart is inclined toward young Christian women and their unique challenges.

Having earned her bachelor of arts in communications from Whitworth University, Jodi's first "real job" was at NavPress

Publishing. She went on to work for Peak Creative and Multnomah Publishers as a copywriter. Now writing in Portland, Oregon, for the Luis Palau Association, Jodi thanks the rain for enhancing her freelance career.

Known as the Word Chef, Jodi enjoys playing with her food (words) and creating concoctions from scratch, but also makes her mark as a skilled slicer and dicer (editor). Magazine articles are her appetizer of choice, and *Who Do You Think You Are* is her first hearty entrée (book).

Jodi enjoys speed walks, deep talks, and hot sauce. She is (still) as single as can be.

About Greater Reach Ministries

Greater Reach Ministries, a 501(c)(3) organization, was incorporated as a nonprofit ministry in 2006. The vision of Greater Reach Ministries is to reach out across the world to lift up women and touch them with a message of hope that inspires and equips them to be all that God made them to be.

Their mission is:

- To help women find value, significance, and identity in Christ
- To equip women to develop their gifts, talents, and passions
- To empower women to engage in fruitful ministry

Their strategy is to partner with the local church to provide real-life teaching coupled with real-life tools to make a real impact in the lives of women around the world. They have three regions of the world in focus: the United States, Eastern Europe, and the Middle East. For more information about this ministry or to have Dr. Beasley speak in your area, please contact the Greater Reach offices at alyssa@greaterreach.com. Their Web address is www.greaterreach.com.